CHILDREN IN TROUBLE: A NATIONAL SCANDAL

BY HOWARD JAMES
STAFF CORRESPONDENT OF
THE CHRISTIAN SCIENCE MONITOR

© 1969 THE CHRISTIAN SCIENCE PUBLISHING SOCIETY   ALL RIGHTS RESERVED

Published by The Christian Science Publishing Society, One Norway Street, Boston, Massachusetts, U. S. A.

Contents

CHAPTER I

'We didn't give him any help'

Even conscientious juvenile authorities admit they often fail
to meet the special needs of their charges. For the less than
conscientious, neglect and even brutality are the
guidelines. The first chapter cites case histories that show the
many roads a youngster travels toward delinquency.

SMALL, BLOND, FRECKLE-FACED
Peter was driving the tractor on a rural
Maine road when his brother fell off and
was killed by a hay baler.

With reason clouded by grief and anger,
the parents openly blamed bright, hard-
working, 15-year-old Peter for the accident.
Peter panicked and ran, staying away three
days. When he returned to school some of
the students began calling him "Killer."

His grades dropped. He gave up sports and
started smoking. Then he did strange, defiant things in class. Things that upset some
of his teachers. Finally he was caught stealing money at school.

It wasn't long before a judge found Peter
delinquent and committed him to Maine's
reform school for boys.

Peter is just one of the thousands of boys
and girls I found locked up. His story, like
that of every child, is unique. Some have
committed appalling crimes. Many have not.
Thousands are sent to reform school by
parents under a law that permits them to
declare their offspring uncontrollable. Other
children simply have no home.

They're not all dangerous

This series focuses on children in trouble.
Not just dangerous young criminals and
tough delinquents, but all children in trouble
— the near delinquents, the mentally retarded, the neglected, the abused, the emotionally disturbed. They number in the
millions.

To protect the children, their real names
are not used in these articles.

This series also looks at what happens to
children when they become entangled in the
juvenile system of justice. Or when they
come in contact with tax-supported agencies
that, at least in theory, help children in
trouble. Special emphasis will be given to

reform schools—places some frustrated professionals cynically call garbage dumps for
unwanted children.

In some states these are places where
children may be brutally beaten. In many
reform schools, as well as jails, boys and
girls are forced into homosexual acts. In
almost all institutions the child lives a cold,
unloving life.

What about Peter?

What will happen to Peter? It is too early
to tell. He is better off than many of the
nation's children in trouble. While Maine's
training school is far from being the nation's
best, it is also far from being the worst.

If all goes well, Peter may not be permanently harmed by the experience — as
many youths are. Yet the possibility of his
graduating from the reform school to an
adult prison is high.

If the typical American could visit children's institutions across the country, he
would be shocked.

Who could expect, in a Massachusetts reform school, to walk, as I did, through
waves of little hands; the hands of boys
seven to nine; hands reaching out, pleading;
children begging for someone to stop and
care.

Who would believe without seeing it, that
a tough, ugly member of the Hell's Angels
could nearly break down and cry in a California reform school when, in a lengthy interview, his mark of shame was exposed:
He could not read.

'We acted as servants'

One must meet 17-year-old Sally to understand these young people. She was in the
Virginia reform school for girls, committed
a week after her mother passed on in 1967
and now serving her second term.

"His mother told the court . . . she didn't want Stan"

Confused, emotionally disturbed Sally tells you how she was once placed in a foster home with five other girls—a farm "where we had to scrub chicken houses and act as servants." One must see Sally, a girl who finds reform-school life more comfortable than much of what she experienced on the outside since her mother's death, to begin to understand.

It is essential to recognize that only a small percentage of the several million children in trouble have committed serious crimes. Obviously, society must be protected from those who have. But experts ask why the millions of children who are not a threat to society — and may in fact have been neglected by their parents — should be treated like hardened criminals.

These millions of youngsters fall into eight often overlapping classifications: (1) the dependent and neglected—including battered children; (2) those considered mentally retarded; (3) the mentally or emotionally disturbed; (4) children with serious school problems; (5) the one-parent child; (6) youngsters with intact families but fighting to survive in big-city slums and other destructive environments; (7) the physically handicapped, and (8) the outright delinquent.

Of course, not all children in these categories are in trouble. But experts point out that those who are need special help and strong adult support. Specific suggestions will be made at various points throughout this series.

The key to the category a child falls into generally depends upon who first becomes concerned with his behavior. What happens to him depends largely on the interest of his parents, and the interest and tolerance of school officials, neighbors, and others who come in contact with the child daily.

On the record

If a child is first noticed by the police, and there is little interest at home, the child probably will end up delinquent. In many police stations, Milwaukee for example, the child's contact with the police is recorded on a card. The contact may be because of a serious crime, or simply because he was out 10 minutes past curfew. The child's record remains in a permanent file until the child reaches age 21, when, in some cities, it may be burned or sealed. In other cities this juvenile police record remains in the files indefinitely.

If the child is first noticed by neighbors, and the behavior is clearly attributed to parental neglect at that time (or the child has broken no laws), then he probably will find his way into the welfare system. This may occur even when the child is as de-

linquent as those noticed by police. Some also eventually will be classified as delinquent, although the process may take longer.

If the child is first noticed by the school, again he may be classified as a delinquent. The schools are even less prepared than welfare departments to deal with problem children (although more schools are beginning to help physically handicapped children and those classified as retarded).

The child who acts strangely and is routed to a mental-health institution may never become caught up in the delinquency system, although he may end up in an institution for life.

Take the case of Stan, from a small town in northwestern Iowa.

His parents, after a bitter battle, were divorced when he was nine. His mother told the court her hands were full with the smaller children and she didn't want Stan. So he was awarded to his father.

Youth's behavior deteriorates

Stan's life was not a happy one. Six years later, both parents remarried, and he was sent back to his mother. She complained that Stan had regular temper tantrums followed by fits.

Again she decided she didn't want him, and in early 1966 Stan was sent to live with his grandparents. They couldn't handle him, and so, in August, 1966, a judge sent him to the state's Annie Wittenmyer Home in Davenport. That institution houses dependent and neglected children, some retarded children, others who are emotionally disturbed, and some delinquents.

There Stan grew more difficult day by day. Finally, on Sept. 5, 1967, he was sent to the Mental Health Institute at Cherokee. In the mental hospital he was placed in quarters with older men. Reports show his behavior grew worse.

Deciding he was not the type of child that should be committed to a mental hospital, authorities sent him to the Woodward State Hospital-School, which handles retarded children and uncontrollable epileptics. (Some doctors believe that Stan has slight brain damage and minor retardation as well as epilepsy because of a skull fracture sustained when he was six months old.)

Woodward officials concluded Stan was "too intelligent" for their program. So he was shipped off to a new institution near Des Moines, the Iowa Methodist Group Home. A few weeks later he ran from there and ended up in court again.

One report in Stan's file states: ". . . none of the services available to children in Iowa are willing or want to deal with this difficult problem."

Solitary confinement

The judge sent Stan back to the Annie Wittenmyer School (an institution which felt totally unprepared to care for him) on May 10, 1968.

By this time Stan was reacting violently to what was happening to him. He was often out of control. Twice he assaulted staff members. Officials feared for the smaller children—some as young as eight and nine—at the coeducational Wittenmyer Home.

The home locked Stan in solitary confinement for weeks. He at least had an outside window, was given something to read, and saw a qualified social worker regularly.

Among other things it was suggested that Stan be sent to the state reform school at Eldora. The mental hospital at Cherokee refused to take him back. Finally he was shipped off to the mental hospital at Mount Pleasant.

Stan was still there as this was written, but there was some indication that he would soon be sent elsewhere.

"We didn't give him any help, and I don't think any one else has," admits James Holmes, superintendent of the Wittenmyer Home.

I found hundreds of Stans scattered across America.

Not all children locked up are legally held.

In Rhode Island I found less than 10 of the children held in the training school were committed there. Their status was a kind of limbo called "FOC"—further order of the court—for months.

Truancy brings detention

Thousands of other children — some as young as seven or eight — spend months, even years behind bars for offenses that would not put an adult in jail for an hour.

Take James, a 13-year-old Negro from near Savannah, Ga. In late January he was sent to a state detention home by a judge to await an opening in a reform school.

James has committed no crime, other than skipping school. He was placed on probation for truancy last spring and was caught skipping again this winter. State officials say none of his eight brothers and sisters has been in trouble, except for frequent absences from school.

The nine children live with their mother and stepfather in an unpainted four-room shack on a farm owned by a doctor. While they have electricity, there is no inside plumbing, and the only heat is provided by a small wood-burning stove in the living room. Total income for the family of 11: the $57 a week earned by the stepfather, a man without any formal education, as a farm laborer. James's mother says she went through 10th grade in a Negro school.

It is clear why the children, despite the acute poverty in the home, have never been in trouble before. James's stepfather is described by a worker for the Georgia State Department of Family and Children Services as "the definite head of the household," a man with "a very warm relationship with his wife and children."

The family regularly attends a Methodist church. And their shack is located in a wooded area with a stream to fish in and plenty of room for the children to play.

The state worker who investigated the case explains the truancy this way: There "seems to be the lack of understanding on the part of the parents of the necessity of attending school regularly. James's [stepfather] never attended school regularly and yet managed to support his family. Consequently, he felt the boys had enough school education and did not think it necessary that they stay in school regularly."

Troubled youngster slapped

There is little or no help for children stumbling along the path to delinquency. Action is seldom taken until it is too late. Parents, welfare departments, and public schools often speed up the delinquency process.

In a New York City public school for troubled youngsters I watched a male teacher hit a youngster in the face when the child failed to stand properly in a line after a class. The teacher didn't know I was watching.

In Milwaukee one 11-year-old child locked in the detention center—a jail for children—by the welfare department was forgotten for three months. Jailing homeless or mistreated children is, unfortunately, a too-common practice. The judge in Milwaukee echoed the words I have heard in other cities: "Somebody should teach the welfare department a lesson by charging them with neglect."

Like adults, many children are locked up to await their court appearance.

The National Council on Crime and Delinquency estimates that "every year in the United States over 100,000 children from 7 to 17 inclusive are held in jails and jail-like places of detention."

And, the council adds, "the significance of this situation is not merely the large number held, or the fact that most of the jails in which they are detained are rated unfit for adult offenders by the Federal Bureau of Prison's Inspection Service, but rather that many of these youngsters did not need to be detained in a secure facility in the first place."

He only needs a home

Some have no family, or a family so inadequate they cannot be returned home.

At the Lyman (reform) School for Boys in Massachusetts I found David, a very depressed youth, sitting head in hands on some steps. Asked why, the tour guide said David, who had no parents, could have been released more than a year ago if the school could only have found a place for him to go. One staff member suggested he should never have been sent by the judge in the first place.

There are thousands of Davids locked up. In several states, training-school superintendents told me they would send a third, even half, of the children home the day they arrived if they could.

Not all institutions are bad. A number are conscientiously doing the best they can with their inadequate staffs and limited budgets. A handful are doing a great deal of good. Others are horrible beyond belief.

In a South Carolina reform school I found, among other things, boys being beaten with fists, rubber hoses, ropes, broken hoe handles and broom handles, and other weapons. Beatings were administered both by staff members and by large bully-boys appointed to do the job.

When a lawyer and state legislator, T. Travis Medlock, learned of these findings, I was invited by a legislative committee to conduct another investigation. When Mr. Medlock and Jack Shivers, who is in charge of juvenile institutions in South Carolina, found my allegations to be true, beatings at the school were stopped and other changes made.

In a Delaware boys' school I found children being hit in the face. This was the authorized institutional policy for disciplining a child, established by an ex-football star of the '40's, Caleb Van Warrington Jr., who has run the school. He publicly called it a "new way" of handling children. The policy was authorized by the Delaware Youth Services Commission. Mr. Warrington was recently promoted to executive director of that commission. Several youngsters, I learned, had punctured eardrums as a result of this practice.

Reporter threatened

A few days later I was asked to return by the youth commission to discuss what I found. Instead of talking, an effort was made to discredit me at the secret meeting held in a motel room. However, Richard Wier, a member of the Delaware Attorney General's staff, was present. He conducted a new investigation and invited me to take part. When we entered the school Mr. War-

rington twice threatened — once in the presence of Mr. Wier — to "get" me.

Since then at least one staff member has been suspended and the slapping policy stopped. The Delaware Senate has ordered the Youth Services Commission to hold a "full inquiry" into the operation of all the state's juvenile detention homes and to report its findings to the Senate by June 30.

Until O. J. Keller, new Florida Youth Commission director, put a stop to it last fall, youngsters in the boys' school at Marianna were brutally beaten with a weighted leather flogging strap.

I found children being beaten in several other states, as will be shown in future articles in this series.

It is common for some professionals dealing with children to deny that these practices exist. Some brazenly lie about it. When provided with evidence that their statements are false, some officials try to justify this by complaining of a lack of money. Many went to great lengths to hide brutality and serious shortcomings from me.

Most offenses are minor

Who are these children in trouble?

I found the average citizen pictures them as gun-toting hoodlums and their molls.

There is little doubt that juvenile crime is a growing problem in the United States.

But the fact is most children in trouble have either skipped school, run away from home, been in a series of fist fights, stolen small quantities of candy or clothing or toys or jewelry, or been caught drinking on several occasions.

Of those held for more serious offenses, most have either stolen cars for a ride or have burglarized closed stores or homes when the owners were out.

Only a very small percent were armed robbers or children who physically harmed others.

Yet frightened citizens are being furnished incomplete information from such agencies as the Federal Bureau of Investigation—information which is easily distorted by their impact in headlines.

In 1967 Prof. Marvin E. Wolfgang, graduate chairman of the Department of Sociology, University of Pennsylvania, wrote in a little-noticed report published by the U.S. Department of Health, Education, and Welfare:

"There is little more than faulty and inadequate official delinquency statistics to answer basic questions about the current extent and character of youth crime."

He continues: "The public image of a vicious, violent juvenile population producing a seemingly steady increase in violent crime is not substantiated by the evidence available."

The Uniform Crime Reports, published by the FBI, often used to show a soaring juvenile crime rate, really only show that more juveniles than adults are being arrested, Professor Wolfgang points out.

"Most police officers agree that it is easier to effect an arrest in cases involving juveniles than in cases involving adults," he explains.

Misleading labels cited

The FBI statistics are based on roughly 30 percent of the serious crimes reported to or uncovered by the police, he adds. That is the percentage solved by arrest. The remaining 70 percent of serious crime reported are never cleared up by police, and so it is impossible to guess how many are committed by adults and how many by juveniles.

"In addition very often crude legal labels attached to many acts committed by juveniles give a false impression of the seriousness of their act," Professor Wolfgang continues.

"For example, a 'highway robbery' may be a $100-theft at the point of a gun and may result in the victim's being hospitalized from severe wounds. But commonly, juvenile acts that carry this label and are used for statistical compilation are more minor.

"Typical in the files of a recent study were cases involving two nine-year-old boys, one of whom twisted the arm of the other in the school yard to obtain 25 cents of the latter's lunch money. This act was recorded and counted as 'highway robbery.'

"In another case, a nine-year-old boy engaged in exploratory sexual activity with an eight-year-old girl on a play lot. The girl's mother later complained to the police who recorded the offense as 'assault with intent to ravish.'

"Nothing now exists in the official published collection of crime statistics to yield better information about qualitative variations of seriousness,' " Professor Wolfgang concluded.

The yearlong study just completed by this newspaper clearly indicates that what Professor Wolfgang said in 1967 remains true in 1969.

Juvenile delinquency is serious. But the American people too often are being frightened and misled. One theory is that it is part of a growing effort to pressure the Supreme Court of the United States into reversing rulings of recent years in the field of juvenile and criminal justice.

The most reliable statistics are seriously outdated, for they are based on 1960 census reports. And the figures show only a fragment of the total picture, since children are

shuffled in and out of institutions daily, and the census is representative of a single day in 1960.

On this representative day in 1960 there were 306,325 Americans under the age of 21 living in various kinds of institutions.

Of these, roughly a third (101,420) were in so-called correctional institutions: 44,366 in reform schools; 28,325 in prisons and reformatories; 17,598 in local jails and workhouses; 9,903 in detention homes (juvenile jails); and 1,228 in centers awaiting placemen in reform schools.

Noncorrectional institutions

Another 73,393 were in welfare homes for dependent and neglected children; 78,333 in homes and schools for mentally handicapped youngsters; and 21,986 in adult mental hospitals and residential treatment centers.

There were 28,380 children in institutions for the physically disabled, with the largest number, 11,207, in homes and schools for the deaf.

A total of 2,813 girls were in homes for unwed mothers on that day in 1960.

It is especially important to note that this is only a fraction of all children in trouble in any category.. Because of constant turnover in some institutions—especially jails and detention homes — the total is many times larger.

Nor are children always as quickly institutionalized as the Maine youth involved in the tractor accident. In fact many who are mentally ill or retarded or are dependent and neglected may wait for months or years for bed space. Meanwhile, others find themselves in reform schools.

At the reformatory at Cheshire, Conn.—a prison for youthful offenders—I met Jerry, a tall, thin, white boy of 17, who had become involved with a gang of youths who broke into buildings, stole cars, and committed other offenses throughout Connecticut. He was in the reform school in 1966 and 1967.

Jerry began getting into trouble in Hartford at 8, through the encouragement of his then 10-year-old brother. Both have been involved in crime since then. The brother has also been in the reformatory at Cheshire.

"We used to skip church and steal newspapers and doughnuts out of parked cars," Jerry says.

His parents didn't know

His parents owned a small business that kept both the mother and father busy for long hours, seven days a week. The boys roamed the streets. Because Jerry's older brother fronted for him, the parents didn't suspect. When they finally learned of his criminal behavior and took the time to talk about it, Jerry was beyond their reach. And their approach was always simply to say how bad his behavior made them feel.

By the time he was 13 Jerry "hit it big," finding large amounts of cash in two apartments. Soon he had several other youngsters interested in the easy money.

"Then I decided to stop. I had all I wanted. I even bought a horse and kept him at a riding stable. My folks didn't know. The other kids kept goin' until they got caught. They ratted on me, and I got sent to Meriden [the reform school]."

"After I got out of there I was doin' all right for a couple of months. I started workin' at [a drive-in]. Then I met a kid who had a car, and we used to drive around. One day we were both outa money, and I knew how to get some. We broke into a house. The other kid had done it before. I bought a car with the money, and pretty soon we were breakin' in day after day, month after month. He brought in all his relatives and before we knew it there was about 10 of us. Finally about five of us got caught in an apartment."

Family delinquency

Frequently, entire families are delinquent.

Debbie is an attractive blue-eyed girl of 16 from Lubbock, Texas. I met her in the reform school at Gainesville. It was her third time in—each time for a more serious offense. She has had one illegitimate child.

Her 22-year-old brother was locked up in the boys' school. Her 20-year-old sister, now a divorcee, had been in reform school. So has her 19-year-old sister, who at present is living out of wedlock with a boy. Debbie's 15-year-old brother is skipping school. Only a 10-year-old sister is treading the straight and narrow and "even wants to go to college."

All three of the older girls have had frequent sexual relations with their father. Like her sisters, Debbie was forced to start when she was 12. All have run away from home— as have the brothers.

Her father, often drunk, works as a mechanic in a gas station; her mother clerks in a small store. Debbie's father frequently beats her mother when drunk, and he whips the children severely when they misbehave. This simply drives them out of the home and into more serious troubles.

Although whites comprise the largest single group among delinquents, the problem knows no racial, religious, or even regional boundaries.

The number of middle-class and upper-middle-class children finding their way into public institutions is on the upswing.

Experts attribute this to many things: the mushrooming drug problem; the costliness today of enrolling troubled children in special private institutions; the greater number of middle-income families than before; increasing middle-class divorces; a breakdown of traditional values, plus the high mobility of youngsters in the age of the two-car family. Suburban teen vandalism grows day by day.

Take Carol, a rather plain girl of 16, who, before being locked up, lived with her middle-class parents in Seattle. I found her in one of Washington State's training schools.

Trouble traced to father

She had been there five months, after being arrested for pushing dope and for smoking marijuana. She had never been arrested until she became involved with drugs while dating an older boy who had been in a great deal of serious trouble. He was sent to reform school four or five times for car theft, armed robbery, assault, and other offenses, and has graduated to the adult prison system.

When Carol was nine she was sexually assaulted by her father. Her mother found out and sent Carol to live with her grandmother for a while.

"My experience with my father made everything rotten," she told me. "I felt dirty, and I guess I still don't have too high of an opinion of myself."

This is why she became involved with a boy in trouble. She didn't feel she was good enough for better boys.

Beth is a white girl of 15. I met her in the Waxter Children's [detention] Center in Maryland, not far from the nation's capital. Beth, who is a chubby girl, had run away from home. She had been in the detention center for two months when I met her. I asked why she had been there so long and was told her middle-class parents said they didn't want her.

Rural children as well as those from cities have problems.

Bill comes from a small town in Idaho. He was nine when he was first sent to the reform school at St. Anthony. When I met the blond youngster he was 12.

Bill, who is small for his age, has not seen his father, an ex-convict, for several years. His mother, brother, and sister are on welfare, as is his grandmother. His family moves frequently, and there is town gossip about his mother—although she is also reported to have serious eye trouble and a heart condition.

When Bill was placed in a foster home in 1965 he "tore it apart."

One Idaho official told me Bill was "learning a good deal of deviant behavior" while in the reform school. And another expects the boy to remain in the institution "until he is old enough to go to the state pen."

In a two-week period before being returned to the reform school, he was accused of enough commotion in his home community to keep the town angry at him for years.

Delinquent, or just neglected?

A judge reports that Bill was accused of: "breaking the limb of a neighbor's cherry tree; taking empty pop bottles off of a truck; fighting; shoplifting; stealing toys; running through a vegetable garden, pulling up vegetables; entering a dairy and taking small change; stealing a purse from a woman at a laundry; spraying water around a gas station, followed by cussing; getting caught with his hands in a barbershop cash register; getting caught with his hands in a cash register in a laundry; vandalism at a neighbor's; climbing a peach tree, and sassing the woman who told him to stop picking green fruit; and hanging around the railroad station, climbing aboard trains [among other things]."

Are children like Bill really delinquent?

Or are they actually more dependent or neglected?

Experts agree there is a very fine line—often blurred—between the neglected child and one accused of being delinquent. This is also true of those classified as mentally retarded or considered emotionally unstable.

Reform schools are usually poorly equipped to deal with most of those committed because of this. Most courts, police departments, jails, and institutions just muddle along.

In South Carolina I met Peanuts, a tiny Negro youth who tests out at an IQ of 36, and functions at the level of a three-year-old. He was in a reform school with serious delinquents—a brutal school that reminds one of Nazi concentration camps.

In the reform school in New Hampton, N. Y., I met Al, a 15-year-old Negro who was identified as "definitely retarded," and was treated accordingly.

Yet I found Al easy to talk to. And just as our interview ended a staff member entered and gave Al a small trophy. I asked him what it was for and he smiled and handed it to me.

Al was the chess champ of the reform school.

A policeman takes no chances as he frisks two youths in the regulation manner.

CHAPTER II

'Children cannot be stored...'

Today across America, jail-like centers often house youngsters
whose only crime is that they have no home. Usually
overcrowded, dirty, and poorly staffed, these facilities merely
provide "storage" that degrades and brutalizes.
This chapter spotlights some of these institutions.

THE RUSSET JAIL UNIFORM NEARLY touched 14-year-old Ellen's ankles. It wasn't that the uniform was so big; rather that she was so small.

On the March afternoon that I met Ellen, a vivacious little pixie, she had been locked in the jail (which, while quite clean, reminded me, with its brown tile walls and toilets, of a public restroom equipped with beds and a table) for two weeks and two days.

Ellen was in the county jail in Rock Island, Ill., because the public welfare department put her there — with the approval of a circuit judge.

A social worker had filed a petition stating that the little girl was "in need of supervision" and should be taken from her dull, plodding mother. Since there seemed no place else to keep her until the judge could hear the case, she was jailed.

At the hearing, which took place the afternoon I was there, the judge decided the social worker was right, and returned Ellen to jail until he could find another place to send her.

Ellen, who has never known her father, has often stayed away from home until late at night. It was reported that she has been picked up by men from time to time, and it was hinted that Ellen was sexually used by these men — although no proof was offered in court.

'I just hated school'

When I talked to Ellen she was bouncing around the jail excitedly.

"I was so happy today," she bubbled, unable to sit still. "I got out of this place for court, and I'm gonna go tomorrow to Lutheran Hospital. They're gonna find out about my IQ."

I asked her about school.

"Oh, I just hated school," she said, as if

it were in the distant past. "In kindergarten I missed 125 days. In first grade I was absent two months. I missed 'bout two months in second. In third I only went four months the whole year. I played hooky like that most all the way through school. But I was real sick once, too. I should be in eighth grade, but they put me in seventh. I guess they did that because I've missed so much."

If Ellen is not found to be retarded (she was bright and quick when I talked to her), the court will try to place her in Namequa Lodge, a home run by the county. Final decision will be based on an interview with those who run the institution, and on bed space.

Wherever Ellen is placed, if she runs away she may be sent to reform school. Even if she does not run, her jail experience has had a negative impact on her.

For in jail Ellen has become a close friend of 18-year-old Betty Ann, a member of a local sex and motorcycle gang. Betty Ann likes to talk about having had intercourse with 25 different men and boys—often with several in one night.

Now Ellen says excitedly: "When I get out of jail I'm going to join a motorcycle gang, too—I want to do that more than anything in the world."

Repeated thousands of times

There are thousands of Ellens in jail, or in jaillike juvenile detention centers in the United States.

The National Council on Crime and Delinquency (NCCD) estimates that more than 100,000 children are held in these facilities each year. A total of 2,800 counties (93 percent) in the United States have only jails or jaillike facilities for holding youngsters in trouble with the law, according to NCCD data.

"... like ripe peaches in a warm cellar"

"Detention," the NCCD asserts, "even if it is only overnight, may contribute to delinquency by confining some children unnecessarily. These youngsters, when placed with more sophisticated law violators, are given additional delinquency status."

Yet some system of holding children in trouble is necessary. Some youngsters are so violent or are so caught up in criminal behavior that they must be restrained to protect both themselves and society. Others must be protected from parents and other adults who mistreat them mentally or physically or both.

But the key is in who is held and how. "Children cannot be stored without deterioration," NCCD experts explain, "unless program and staff are provided to make the experience a constructive one." Too often all society provides is storage—like ripe peaches in a warm cellar.

Take Tina, a little girl of 12, half white and half Negro. I found her locked in a cell in the Yakima, Wash., detention center (better described as a juvenile prison).

Jailed for her 'own safety'

Officials said Tina grew up in a shack, living off garbage dump pickings. She was jailed for her "own safety" after being sexually molested by an uncle.

She might better be held in a foster home, but none is available.

The Yakima detention center is probably the cleanest facility of its kind in America. And it can best be described as awful. It is the classic example of what the experts say damages children and causes crime—even while the public thinks it is being protected, or that the children are being helped.

In Yakima, children spend an average of 20 hours a day in solitary confinement awaiting court action. During this time they have absolutely nothing to do but sit behind thick cell doors. They're not even permitted to read.

Don Rolstad, director of the Yakima County Juvenile Department, calls the situation tragic, but adds that it is better now than in the past. Today only dependent and neglected children 12 years or older are held at the center.

"Until recently we had kids two, three, four, and five years old locked up," he says. "I fought with the welfare department four years before we could change that."

Children are not properly screened as they should be, he says, because "I've got one person doing the work of four." Many youngsters spend weekends in the center because no one is authorized to send them home.

"We know what's happening to these kids," he says. "A lot of them were rejected and depressed before they came. And then we put them in a cell, and it's like locking them up and throwing away the key."

Since my visit there last fall Mr. Rolstad has been negotiating with the local school district, hoping to get classes started in the detention home. So far efforts have failed. A few women volunteers come in to work with girls, but most do not come regularly.

Perhaps most shocking in Yakima is the fact that of the roughly 1,200 children jailed there each year, fewer than 300 are found to be delinquent by the court.

It is obvious from the Yakima example that the quality of the institution cannot be judged solely on the condition of the building.

Clue to overcrowding

Yet when youngsters demolish cells and otherwise damage the building week after week it is fairly certain that the institution is overcrowded, creates hostility in agressive youngsters, and has an inadequate staff and activity program. (It may also mean children classified as mentally ill are being held for long periods of time.)

The superintendent of the Audy Home in Chicago refused to let me study it except on a "guided group tour," which I rejected. The home has been called a brutal place by juvenile experts such as Joseph R. Rowan of the John Howard Association, a nonprofit prison-reform and correctional service organization.

In Atlanta I found a horrible detention home behind an attractive facade in the shadow of the new $18 million sports center, and near a multimillion-dollar expressway complex.

The home is constantly overcrowded. On the February morning I was there 191 children were locked up. Built for 144, it houses delinquent children, retarded youngsters, and those classified as dependent and neglected, including babies too small to walk. All children over 10 years of age are mixed together. Thus those who have been abandoned or mistreated by parents, and who have never committed a crime, are locked in with tough hoodlums.

Building damaged

The boys' section is constantly being torn apart by angry youths, who sometimes seem in control of the institution. One boy was stabbed with a plastic tooth-brush handle that had been rubbed into a stiletto on a cement wall.

Toilets are constantly overflowing as youngsters plug them with toilet paper and anything else they can get their hands on.

Rooms were built for one child, but they house two. Youngsters on the upper bunks kick the ceilings out. Security screens are constantly being ripped from windows. There is only one man to make repairs, and he is always days behind in his work.

I found one boy locked in a solitary confinement cell without a bed. (This is all too common around the nation.) The room reeked with the stench of urine and feces. Garbage, apparently several days old, littered the floor. The youngster insisted he was kicked in the stomach because he refused to follow orders. The guard, a mammoth man, contended that the child was pushed, not kicked.

Two day rooms unfurnished

There are four day rooms, but because of lack of finances only two have been furnished. Classroom space is totally inadequate. Thus most youngsters have nothing to do but sit for hours each day.

I saw one boy of about 12 or 13 sitting with his hand in his mouth. He has, I was told, an IQ of around 40, which means he is severely retarded. He is not dangerous, they added, except to himself. Why is he locked up?

"He just drifts around town," it was explained. "He isn't dangerous. It's just that nobody can control him."

Downstairs, in a less-depressing section, the small dependent children are housed. But there are only six inches between the double bunks that line the girls' dormitory. In the room for babies there are 9 cribs.

"We try not to get youngsters under a year old," an official explained. "But we have problems on this with the welfare department. We can't get them to provide emergency care."

John S. Langford, a conscientious juvenile judge, was handling the entire Atlanta court caseload alone until Jan. 1. He said he is appalled at conditions in the dentention home.

"We have been begging and pleading for more space," he says.

Young sculptor met

Girls are better off than the boys, but not much. A little 11-year-old white girl who was pregnant was locked in with the rest. Frightened, angry, resentful, she tried to assault a matron and take the keys. Some girls have been held in Atlanta's children's jail for a year. One was waiting five months for an opening in a reform school.

During bad weather there is no place for the children to exercise. The outside wall in the play area was recently raised from 8 to 11 feet to cut down on escapes. A gym will be built eventually.

It was here that I met Millard, a very talented 16-year-old, who was sculpturing a bust of the Rev. Martin Luther King Jr. in clay in the art room — one of the best features of the institution, though one which obviously could be developed further. A sensitive boy, Millard was placed in a foster home four years ago because of parental neglect. The oldest of five children, his brothers and sisters are scattered in other foster homes.

Millard was jailed with some young Atlanta hoodlums by the welfare department because he had arguments with a foster mother. Yet he had not broken the law. The woman simply decided she couldn't deal with a rebelling teen-ager.

After being locked up a month he was returned to the same foster home that had refused to keep him. Mrs. Helen Fuller, the excellent probation officer who handled the case while Millard was locked up, points out that the youth is now a full month behind in school, and it is "touch and go" whether he will stay in or drop out.

The same day I met Millard, I found Beth, a beautiful white girl of 15, sobbing outside the Atlanta courtroom. Her father, a middle-class executive who travels for a large corporation, had insisted she be locked up.

Until this school year Beth had been a straight A student, although she was deeply disturbed by her parents' unpleasant divorce two years ago. The father had been given custody of all the children.

Things were not right at home, and Beth's 13-year-old brother has started to get into trouble. Beth had run away in the middle of the night; stolen her father's car; gotten drunk; and had relations with boys. Psychiatrists said she stole compulsively.

The father wanted Beth sent to a mental hospital.

Instead Beth had a complete psychiatric examination. As a result, the court ruled that both she and her father needed psychiatric help. The judge added that a mental hospital was not the answer.

Returned after five weeks

After being locked up for five weeks, she was returned to her father. No one can force the father to seek help. In addition to her other problems, Beth is now far behind in school.

Her probation officer said she expects to see Beth back in the detention center soon.

As in Atlanta, many detention centers are overcrowded.

Los Angeles's Juvenile hall processes up to 2,000 children a month and occasionally they will be as young as six years. While there is space for 400 boys and 162 girls, the day I was there I found more than 500 boys and 200 girls locked in. On an earlier visit

I had found more than 200 youngsters sleeping on mats on the floor. I was told this is not uncommon.

The Los Angeles detention home, like most, feels prisonlike. All those housed there have been accused of delinquency, although some are considered mentally retarded or mentally ill. A few youngsters are held three, four, five, or even six months, usually awaiting a place to go.

There is a school on the grounds, but far too little play space. A second swimming pool was under construction when I was there. But most children live in drab cell-like rooms, and there are sleeping mats stacked in every unit for the overflow.

Back in 1961, adequate detention homes were spending between $10 and $20 a day on each child, according to the National Council on Crime and Delinquency. Yet in 1969, this newspaper found children in jails that budgeted less than $1.50 a day per child.

Some detention homes and jails do not measure up to state minimum living conditions. In Davenport, Iowa, the detention home failed to pass state inspection five years running before it finally was shut down Jan. 1 through the urging of concerned citizens and Judge Bertram B. Metcalf.

Children under 10 now are taken to a church-run home, while the older youngsters go to a state-run school for dependent and delinquent children located in Davenport. Dependent and delinquent children are mixed. Yet most of these children go to their own home school every day.

One is forced to ask: If the children can be trusted to go to public school, why must so many be locked up?

Judge overworked

But a few Davenport area youngsters still go to the Scott county jail. And the typical child may be held several days or weeks because Judge Metcalf is so unbelievably overworked.

In many jails—especially those where the sheriff is paid so much per inmate per day —food is horrible. For the sheriff is able to pocket whatever he can save on meals.

In one South Carolina jail youngsters were fed thin soup or beans. In another they got only cornbread and powdered milk for their evening meal seven days a week.

This policy also encourages locking children up, for the more inmates, the more the sheriff can make.

It is rather common for boys to be homosexually assaulted by adults in jails. This happens frequently in Chicago and Philadelphia, among other cities. Yet in most states jail is where boys over 16 usually are held—even if they are small or weak.

Carl was 19 years old, a college student and the son of an oil-company executive stationed overseas. A small, thin youth, he was arrested in a stolen car. He eventually found his way to the county jail in Albuquerque, N.M. For two weeks he was locked up with 18 men, fought with them for several days to avoid being gang-raped.

Finally won a move

Carl was eventually able, through a lawyer, to get moved into the juvenile detention, where he had been held five weeks when I met him.

While the Albuquerque dentention home is old and not very clean, it is run by a pleasant woman who may well do more to rehabilitate the children in the days or weeks she has them than the best reform schools can do in months. Mrs. Eula Farrow does it with little help or money and has lived in the center for 17 years. Her population runs to 350 children a month.

Sometimes children enter voluntarily. Not long ago, a boy from a middle-class home rang the bell and she let him in, notifying the parents.

As in Davenport, Iowa, a number of children go by bus from the detention home to the public schools.

One of the nation's better detention homes can be found in Wilmington, Del. Called Bridgehouse, the facility is more homelike than most. It was neither overcrowded nor understaffed the day I was there. The difference in Delaware, as elsewhere, is the quality of staff, length of stay, and use of the facility.

One of the nation's most unpleasant detention homes is found in Memphis, Tenn.

Inadequate library

It reminds one of an adult prison. Children are under the supervision of uniformed guards. Some live in traditional prison cells —inner rooms that look out on a corridor with windows beyond. A metal bed is attached to the wall. Cells have a steel bench and desk. Children, when they are locked in, leave their shoes and other clothing outside. This is to prevent them from hanging themselves. Others sleep in dormitories with beds roughly a foot apart.

The library is small and inadequate. Uniformed boys sit for hours in a day room where they can either read or watch television, but where talking is not permitted. Others work, keeping the place clean. There is some recreation twice a day. No attempt is made to help the youngsters keep up with their schoolwork, as is the case in the better facilities around the country.

Fortunately a separate institution houses

most dependent and neglected children if they have not broken the law.

A few states have taken steps to resolve the problem of where and how to house children in trouble by building regional detention centers. Unfortunately this is only a partial answer.

Children must travel miles to court. They are held long distances from their families. This curbs visiting. These centers are subject to the same flaws found in local detention centers in that they often are crowded with little positive happening to the child. Staffs well may be inadequate. Many of these centers are overcrowded and overused, and state legislatures are seldom more liberal with their funds for child caring than are local units of government.

In Massachusetts the regional detention homes — especially the one in Boston — have been under heavy criticism for these reasons.

Severe treatment meted out

I discovered that the overflow from these institutions was being moved into the training schools. And in the Lyman (reform) School for Boys near Worcester, Mass., I found children being held for court locked in the institution's punishment cottage with the school's troublemakers. Treatment is severe and punitive in this cottage.

It was first denied that this was happening by state officials in Boston. When I proved to them that I was correct, I was told a directive was being sent out to change the practice.

The detention center at Worcester is one of the rare institutions where statistics are gathered:

More than 95 percent are white youngsters —mostly sons and daughters of blue-collar workers. In the eight years the center has been open, between 3,000 and 4,000 youngsters have been locked in. Built for 25 children, it often holds 40 on a typical day, says Paul Leahy, the superintendent.

The most recent study shows that of the boys brought in, slightly less than half (47.1 percent) live with both parents.

The largest number of boys—16.3 percent — were brought in as runaways. The next largest group—15.9 percent—were charged with larceny, while 15.6 percent had stolen a car, usually for a ride rather than to sell it or strip it. Parents had locked up 11.5 percent of those held under the "stubborn-child" statute. Drunkenness locked up 7.9 percent. Another 7.2 percent were school truants. Five percent were charged with breaking and entering, while 1.1 percent had been accused of assault with a deadly weapon.

The poorer the neighborhood, the more

youngsters were locked up — and the more often they were returned to detention.

Even this does not really tell the whole story.

At 10:14 on the night I was there Sharon, a slender girl was brought in by the police. She had 50 cents in her pocket; hadn't eaten for some 48 hours; had turned herself in after wandering the streets for three weeks.

Parents long separated

Her mother and father have been separated for several years, and her mother is now living out of wedlock with a very unpleasant man. Both are heavy drinkers, and home life for the six children has become intolerable since he arrived.

At age 10 she was raped in a wooded area by a 17-year-old boy, and "after that I didn't want to live anymore because my mother acted as if she thought it was my fault it happened."

Yet her grades are above average in school.

Sharon really didn't want to run away. In fact she walked the streets, trying to be noticed by policemen, so she could be taken to court "so I could get into a foster home."

After three weeks of walking past policemen she finally called her mother's welfare worker, who suggested that she turn herself in.

"A child *has* to be arrested to get in here," Mr. Leahy, head of the detention center explained.

Unfortunately Sharon is not assured of a foster home now. Rather she may well be returned home by the court, or may find herself locked up in a reform school.

Georgia also has regional detention centers. One of the best was opened in Rome, Ga., just below Chattanooga, Tenn., on Nov. 20, 1967. An attractive modern building, there are two pianos in the large recreation room, plus Ping-pong and pool tables. Youngsters are permitted to play with old typewriters, work with yarn, read, and listen to radio or watch television.

Of the 500 who have passed through the center, 88 percent have been white; 12 percent Negro, says C. D. Rampley, the superintendent.

Often held for weeks

I found the center staff to be better than most. Yet in one report I read how an 11-year-old Negro girl was whipped with a belt when she misbehaved. I found several girls locked in their room for hours because during a meal they "looked at the boys" who eat in the same dining area.

Youngsters are held for long stays: days and sometimes weeks waiting for court and months for a reform-school opening. And many, had they been picked up by the police in a major city, might not have been locked up at all.

John, a 14-year-old Negro, had shoplifted a pair of gloves with his 12-year-old brother, who is also locked in the center. He said he needed the gloves because the weather turned cold and "Mamma gets social security, but she drinks it up and don't feed us much and don't buy us clothes." He has been in trouble before, once for taking a bicycle gear and twice for "fightin' and cussin'."

He much prefers the detention center to home.

"It's better here than home. Some mornin' I get up, don't get no food. I don't have money to pay for lunch or nothin'. They used to give us a lot of free lunches, but they don't this year. I come back to the house. She still don't give us anything. She's layin' in bed drunk and the house is all nasty and dirty. She has lots of men in the house. Right now she got a man stayin' with her that's been on the chain gang."

How does John do in school?

"I can read a little, but sometimes I have eye trouble. I look at somethin' and I can't see, so I shake my head a little bit. The doctor says I got infection. My brother [age 12] does better in school than I do."

The Rome detention center is fortunate because it does not get many of the angry, bitter youths that are ripping up the Atlanta detention homes. "We get a different breed of child," Mr. Rampley explains.

He is at least partly right, but perhaps underestimates the importance of the way children are treated in relationship to the way they act. This is most obvious in New York State, where I observed tough ghetto youngsters in their upper teens working happily in knee-deep snow in a Division for Youth forest camp. Some of these youngsters had been in deep trouble in New York City and were behavior problems in the detention complex in the Bronx. It was the staff and setting that made the difference.

New York City's Youth House, which holds youngsters from 7 to 16, has often been described as a "hell hole" by concerned citizens.

The staff is generally poor. There are at least two reasons: Pay is extremely low, and thus those who can't find a job elsewhere are too often hired. Nor are staff members tested before they are hired.

There is little status in the job. The dedicated men and women are maligned with the worst by public generalization.

Some of the youngsters are held for nine months to a year in this jaillike facility as they await placement in institutions.

"Some kids come here six or seven times for serious things and they go back home, while another kid has to stay here for playing hooky," another employee complains.

In the girls' section of the detention complex there have been several riots.

Older youths—those between the ages of 16 and 21—are carted off to a prison on Rikers Island, where they are herded into cell blocks like cattle.

"We have a design capacity of about 1,800," says Morris Oslyn, the deputy warden, "but we have had a population as high as 3,200. They come in anywhere from 5 minutes to 4 months or more to await court action. We have three teachers for 16- and 17-year-olds, and they go to school about 3 hours a day, but it hardly begins to touch our needs."

There is really no rehabilitation program at Rikers Island for those awaiting a court appearance. Young men simply go from bad to worse as they mill around the cellblock with little to do for days, weeks, months.

The noise level is so high, the towering cellblock so depressing, and the humanity so dense that after half an hour a visitor feels crushed, overwhelmed. It is like being caught in a stockyard stampede with nowhere to run.

Others even worse

There are other jails and prisons as bad or worse.

I found 175 boys between the ages of 16 and 18 locked in the House of Correction in Philadelphia. The iron-barred cells were filthy, and the paint was peeling.

Connecticut is talking about tearing down its old jails—and with good reason. Little change has taken place in them since the Civil War.

Boys in the Hartford jail pass through a series of steel doors to reach the four-tiered cages where they are kept for days and weeks awaiting court action. Until recently there was not even a shower in the section where they are held.

Seattle's dentention home is a tolerable jail at best, but when children act up they are thrown in a basement dungeon. Joe, a 13-year-old white boy was one of those I found in a cell in the basement.

"I don't got any parents," he told me. "My parents are dead. But I been with three sets of foster parents."

Joe has been locked up 11 times, usually for fighting or refusing to obey. Already he has "been kicked outa school." Frightened, hostile, feeling unloved, he strikes out at people, sometimes with fists, sometimes with words. And each time he has been placed in the center he has done something to get placed in the basement cell—a cement room with only a steel cot and a blanket.

The center is overcrowded, and often boys wind up sleeping on the gym floor.

Walk through another door off the central upstairs corridor, and you discover pathetic toddlers and older girls who have never broken the law. These children are better treated, but must not only face the severance of family ties, but the stigma of being held in the detention home.

Like most children's jails, the detention home in Dallas is an awful place. The new addition being built will help cut down overcrowding, but it will not change the atmosphere.

Because Texas institutions for the mentally retarded are jammed, children in this category are sometimes locked up here for six months or a year.

Positive approach

But normal children here who have not broken the law are among the best treated in the nation. About 100 yards west of the detention home is a welfare-department-run shelter care home. Children under 10 who are accused of delinquent acts are also held in shelter care—a beautiful new building with a gentle, kindly staff.

William E. Portwood, the social worker in charge of the center, believes in "meaningful structure" (rules, discipline, adult attention), but is able to control the children without beating them or locking them in solitary confinement for long periods.

Every possible effort is made to return the child home, or place the youngster with relatives. If this fails, an attempt is made to find a foster home. Failing this, a child may end up in an institution.

Buildings make a difference. A child held behind steel bars will act as if he is in prison because he *is* in prison. Youngsters from big-city slums, who have had to fight to survive, may well be tougher, more violent, than their rural counterparts. But the key to decent detention is decent staff. That plus community concern.

This is the reason Salt Lake City's detention center is better than many, despite occasional overcrowding.

I spent a Saturday there with Claude C. Dean, who treated children like a kindly grandfather. The children responded openly, honestly.

Salt Lake City is fortunate in having a strong and growing citizen-volunteer program.

But the real solution is to find ways to prevent delinquency so that children's jails can be closed.

Children in trouble need special help

CHAPTER III

Do children get their 'day in court'?

Frequently juvenile-court judges must act as substitute parents
for youngsters whose own parents have failed them. Yet,
too often these judges are no better equipped to help than
were the "delinquent" parents. The following chapter
examines the shortcomings of juvenile courts and suggests
ways to improve them.

IF A SOUTH DAKOTA MOTHER LOCKED her daughter in a closet for weeks. . . .

If a Connecticut father forced his son to skip school. . . .

If California parents made a disturbed or retarded child associate with hoodlums seven days a week. . . .

If a Virginia mother saw to it that her daughter was placed in an environment that encouraged homosexuality. . . .

Or if a Delaware or Indiana father turned his son over to men who punctured the boy's eardrums or beat him with a leather flogging paddle until he was black and blue. . . .

Most of these parents would be condemned by the community — even charged in court with criminal neglect.

Yet, too often that is what thousands of judges — serving under the law as substitute parents (parens patriae) — do every time they dump children behind bars. Some of these children have never even committed a crime.

Visits are few or misleading

Few judges visit reform schools or jails. Those who do, however, often complain they are given nice little tours than gloss over the actual conditions. Some of these facilities are so frightful that forward-looking correctional officials like O. J. Keller, head of the Florida Youth Commission, call them "schools for crime."

Yet judges across the country keep shipping children off to these institutions—and then wonder why the crime rate soars.

Not only do some distressed experts suggest that judges should be charged with neglect (along with schools and welfare departments) but it is evident that thousands of judges who demand that children either obey the law or go to jail blatantly ignore the law themselves.

Too often, youngsters in trouble never get the benefit of legal counsel.

In a majority of states judges interviewed have never read the Gault decision handed down in 1967 by the Supreme Court of the United States to protect juveniles. Or else they ignore it.

That decision affirmed that children have the same constitutional rights as adults— that they must not be forced to incriminate themselves, that the court must provide the child a lawyer if his family cannot afford one, and that the child's lawyer must be allowed to cross-examine witnesses.

Many Ohio judges have openly defied the Supreme Court decision in statements made to fellow judges at meetings of the National Council of Juvenile Court Judges.

At a seminar for judges at the University of Minnesota last summer a Monitor reporter was asked to participate by interviewing an Ohio judge on closed-circuit television. This judge admitted before his colleagues that he "ignored" Supreme Court rulings in some cases while demanding that children obey the law to the letter.

Action unknown to parents

Many juvenile courts are beset by long delays. Sometimes children are locked up for weeks or months. Judges say the Gault decision, where it is being observed, has drastically slowed down hearings because youngsters now have lawyers.

Part of the problem is a shortage of juvenile judges. In some cities, children are locked up because judges hold juvenile hearings only once a week.

In South Carolina children are too often sent to reform schools without their parents knowing it. Officials there told me that a child may be picked up at night, jailed, taken before a justice-of-the-peace or other minor magistrate early in the morning, and hauled handcuffed to the reform school before lunch.

Training-school officials then call the parents at home to tell them their children will be locked up for several months, according to George O. Compton, superintendent of the South Carolina School for Girls.

He tells how an officer came in from Myrtle Beach a few years ago with five boys from "substantial families" living in the neighboring state of North Carolina. The boys were accused of siphoning gasoline from a car so they could return home. It took lawyers "three or four months" to get the boys released and home.

Even with full-time, thoughtful juvenile judges problems develop. In the Family Court in Providence, R.I., children are almost never committed to the reform school. And yet the reform school is full! Some children are held FOC (further order of the court) for a year or more without being found delinquent.

The day I was there only 5 of the 186 children in the reform school (boys and girls) had been legally committed.

Many judges and lawyers interviewed across the nation believe the Rhode Island policy of holding children in this manner, without formal commitment, is illegal.

The court's theory seems to be this: If the child is sent to the reform school as a delinquent, then he must face this stigma for life. But if he is simply held FOC, never having been legally declared delinquent, the child's reputation is protected.

This procedure also gives the court final say over when the youngster is released. Joseph P. Devine, who was a very creative superintendent of schools before becoming head of the Juvenile Correctional Institutions in Rhode Island, has started one of the most exciting, creative programs for behavioral change in the country.

Yet, he has to struggle to make it work because the court retains control of the children.

To avoid rigid rules and prevent such brutal practices as flogging, progressive reform schools use a system of rewards for good behavior. Rewards are withdrawn when children misbehave. Many juvenile authorities say the ultimate reward is early release from the institution. This the Rhode Island reform-school authorities cannot use under FOC.

In some states some judges ship children to reform school without the child ever appearing in court.

In the State of Washington a number of children in the reform schools told me this. It was so unbelievable I checked it out; not only did the superintendent of one school say that it was true, he even produced court records to prove it.

Many judges threaten a child with commitment in a way that undermines the reform school. At the same time some judges appear stupid to the children.

"The judge kept telling me how horrible this place [the reform school] was and he said he was gonna send me here if I didn't straighten out," said one New York inmate. "Then when he finally decided I was bad enough to send me up he told me that it wasn't such an awful place after all, and that he was really helping me. What a jerk!"

Driveway commitment

In Ames, Iowa, I found that a youthful probation officer had a young secretary who attended a beer party in a nearby town. There she saw a boy under suspended commitment. She immediately called her employer, who picked up the boy and hauled him to the home of District Judge Ed Kelley. Judge Kelley signed the commitment papers in his driveway. The probation officer confirmed that this happened. Judge Kelley became angered when asked about the case and would only say that "the kid had a full hearing."

Several Iowa judges and lawyers told me later that Judge Kelley was one of the state's best judges.

The nation's leading juvenile judges—men like William S. Fort of Eugene, Ore.—believe that as a result of the Gault decision a hearing must be divided into two parts: the adjudicative hearing and the dispositional hearing.

During the first hearing the judge determines if he has jurisdiction in the case and decides whether the child is delinquent. At this hearing judges who adhere to Gault follow rules a little like those in the criminal court—listening as objectively as possible to evidence.

Children prejudged?

Many judges ignore this. In some cities a prehearing investigation is conducted by probation officials, and before a child appears in court the judge sits in his chambers and listens to the probation officer's views. Then he enters the courtroom and faces the child.

Lawyers in Dover, N.H., Dallas, and in hundreds of other cities complain about this.

Many of the better juvenile courts do have probation officers prepare reports. But this information is not used until the child is found delinquent on evidence. And often the information is not gathered until after the child is found to be delinquent, since a probation officer asking questions about a child at school and in his neighborhood puts a stigma on the child.

Most experienced juvenile judges feel such a report is essential to decisionmaking. If a child has a somewhat stable home, then the child may be put on probation. But when the father is gone and the mother is an alcoholic, or the child is having trouble in school, the judge may send that child to reform school. Thus the child's future is tied to the kind of home he comes from.

Right to counsel ignored

Even the screening that goes on prior to a hearing before a judge may be unjust. Some court official — usually a probation officer—listens to the police, a neighbor, or parent describe the child's offense and then decides whether the child should go to court. He actually acts as a judge holding a preliminary hearing. Since he is often picked by the judge, who has some measure of confidence in his ability, the children who pass this screening enter the court under a cloud.

The Gault ruling was supposed to guarantee a child a lawyer—even if the state must pay for one—if the child is likely to be locked up. And yet I have talked to many judges who argue that their community cannot afford it.

There is little question that if teams of lawyers went to the nation's reform schools today looking for illegally held youngsters they could empty many within a week.

Max B. Harrison is a busy lawyer as well as juvenile judge in Blytheville, Ark. (His brother is circuit judge.) He has not studied Gault; could not even recall what cities his state's reform schools are located in. He says his hearings are "very informal" and "we get most of our referrals either from another court or a peace officer."

99% admit guilt

"They have already made a determination of guilt," he says. "Then the juvenile officer gets information from the family, church, and school records. We hold a hearing, and the probation officer relates information about the law and the violation. He presents it to me. If it is a larceny he tells me the facts.

"Ninety-nine out of a hundred admit their guilt anyway. If somebody charged with larceny said they didn't do it, then I'd hear the evidence and decide whether they did it or not. Now, we're generally ill-equipped to do this. The juvenile officer is not an attorney, and he's not familiar with the laws of evidence or procedure.

"I don't know his [the probation officer's]

background, but he is a very conscientious man, and he does have 11 years' experience.

"We're not equipped for formal hearings. I don't have any authority to appoint anybody [a lawyer] to come up here and represent [children]. Those who want an attorney, well, they can get one. We don't give free counsel; we don't give them Miranda warnings [against self-incrimination]. I think that's mostly taken care of before it gets to me."

Judge Harrison is paid on the basis of the number of hearings he holds — plus travel expense. When I asked him about Supreme Court rulings and other legal procedures, he replied:

"I'm not compensated sufficiently to handle all that detail work. This more nearly approaches a service to the county. Besides it takes so much time I couldn't get anything else done. And it's not punishment anyway."

The nation's best use of lawyers in a juvenile court can be found in Eugene, Ore. There I watched a case in which both the mother and father, who were separated, had lawyers. Among other things, the dispute was over custody of the children. So a lawyer was appointed to represent each child in the case.

But even when special public defenders are hired to represent children, they have too little time to do the job. They whisper briefly with the child in a corner of the courtroom, then walk before the judge — without any investigation or real knowledge of the case. Many are green lawyers cowed by a sometimes domineering judge. The same can be said for many who serve as prosecutors in juvenile cases. Neither the child nor the state is adequately represented in most juvenile courts.

Dual role for judge

As often as not the judge acts as prosecutor—a depressingly unjust practice. Or he assigns the job to a probation worker who later is supposed to win the child's confidence to help him change his ways.

In New York City, judges are politically appointed. Some do an excellent job. Others seem not to care but deal with children like workmen tightening bolts on an assembly line.

New York City Family Courts are among the filthiest in the nation. In Queens the American flag tacked flat behind the bench drags on the floor and is so dirty that one can scarcely tell the white stripes from the red.

Yet New York juvenile judges constantly criticize parents for filthy homes and rail at youngsters for lack of respect.

Many juvenile judges are not even

lawyers. In Marianna, Fla., I met Judge R. Robert Brown who had been a newspaper publisher before taking the bench five days earlier. Concerned, trying to do his best, already he had passed judgment on several youngsters with the help of his clerk, a woman who had worked for the previous judge. Judge Brown openly admits he needs help.

Another nonlawyer handles juvenile cases in Obion County, Tennessee. In addition to being judge, Dan McKinnis is chairman of the county court (the county board); county fiscal officer; director of the budget; county purchasing agent; and probate judge.

He does not have a probation officer to help him, but sends about a dozen children a year to reform school.

"The majority are good children, but they are neglected," he says. "They don't have a proper home environment, and so they get into trouble."

Many judges complain that the law permits them few alternatives to committing children to reform school. Yet, there are judges who are aggressive in searching out what alternatives exist.

Interested judges scarce

Judge Augustus T. Graydon of Richland County, S.C., says, "I would not consider committing any minor to that school [the John G. Richards Reform School] at this time until and unless I am satisfied that the conditions at the school have improved...."

Judge J. McNary Spigner, also from Richland County, had the courage to announce—after wretched conditions were uncovered in the reform schools there by the Monitor's survey—that he would send no more children to the schools until conditions improved.

Unfortunately, the alternatives a juvenile judge has to choose from *are* few. Most communities do not provide halfway houses or foster homes for children in trouble—especially teen-agers. Nor are there many good detention centers for holding youngsters for court. Often those who will work for the low salaries at these centers are unskilled or worse.

It's even hard to find competent judges eager to work in the juvenile field.

Judge tells of frustration

In Seattle four judges rotate—taking six-month terms in juvenile court, while a fifth judge fills in when the presiding judge is gone. This is done, according to Morell E. Sharp (who was on the bench the day I was there), because "the emotional and physical strain is such that six months is about all a judge can take."

Judge Sharp is highly regarded by his fellow judges. He is youthful, bright, polished,

A judge listens.

and knowledgeable in the law. He cares deeply about people. And he is frustrated.

"I feel I am not really accomplishing much when I deal with these children," he explains. "I have a deep feeling of futility. Broken homes, poverty, and other factors found in juvenile cases are outside my jurisdiction. There is so little I can do. We don't even have enough probation staff to do the job. So often we would prefer strict probation to institutionalization."

As in other cities, the juvenile court is not a popular assignment in Seattle "because of the strain."

"Given a choice, and assurance some other judge will do the job properly, most judges request some other assignment," Judge Sharp admits.

"No judge I know really likes working with children," says Judge Harvey Uhlenhopp of Hampton, Iowa. "You work in a gray area all of the time. You never know when you are right.

"Children's problems are never simple. And the juvenile involves the infusion of behavioristic science besides the law. A judge doesn't have time to become an expert. I really don't understand all the things the social workers, psychiatrists, psychologists, and others are saying. The whole field is much too complex."

Juvenile judges are always in danger of becoming embroiled in controversy.

Take the case of Judge Thomas Tang of Phoenix, Ariz. He is one of the most careful, thoughtful judges in the nation. Not long ago he had great public support. Now he is under fire for releasing two boys involved in the death of another boy.

Judge Tang sent both home to their parents instead of ordering them held at the depressing Phoenix detention home. An investigation by the court staff indicated that the boys were not violent and that the parents would be able to control them and assure their appearance in court.

But the Phoenix problem went deeper. Explains another judge: "There is a disgruntled group of former employees [of the detention home] led by a lawyer who was working for the probation department while in law school. The fellow was canned and he carries a grudge and is determined to dump [Judge] Tang."

There is little doubt that juvenile judges have the most difficult job in the whole legal system. A judge's power is awesome. His decisions, made in a few minutes in a courtroom, can make the difference between a life of crime or hardship and a bright future for a child. It is not surprising that few judges want the job.

In Chicago, for example, some of the greenest judges may be assigned to the juvenile court. About the time they begin to understand their job they have enough seniority to ask for an easier assignment.

There are arguments both for and against assigning a judge to a juvenile court for only a few months every year or two. Too short a term results in the judge failing to understand the problems of juveniles. He lacks experience.

Long term found harmful

"Too long a term makes the judge kind of hardened," Seattle's Judge Sharp adds. "He tends to forget the judicial nature of the proceedings and begins shooting from the hip, making decisions not on the basis of law, but on the social aspects."

Whatever the reason, this newspaper found that most judges in the United States avoid juvenile proceedings if they can.

Yet a few persons ask for the assignment. These can be divided into several categories: Judges who have theories about juveniles in trouble and want to experiment; men who want to be a judge, and find less competition in the juvenile field; those who want to build monuments to themselves in the city they live in; lawyers looking for publicity for a variety of reasons; others who can't make a living as lawyers; and those who simply care deeply about children in trouble.

It must be remembered that judges are, after all, only human and for the most part are assigned an almost impossible task. Even those who do much for children are criticized by their own colleagues.

Perhaps best known—and most controversial—is Judge Lester H. Loble of Helena, Mont. Judge Loble has gained wide publicity for pushing a "get tough with kids" policy, locking them in jail, publishing their names in newspapers. He has been in great demand as a public speaker.

Yet in talking to other officials in the Helena courthouse, I was told that he seldom practices the hard line he preaches. One who talks to him gets the impression he is really a very compassionate man.

Says one official who likes Judge Loble, "He wanted to make a national name for himself. He finds kids jobs; tries to keep them out of the reform school; really doesn't lock many in jail; and only publishes a few names—those who commit serious crimes. You can't blame a little man in Montana for wanting to be nationally known."

The official "juvenile crime rate" is down in Helena. But Judge Loble refuses to take cases that show up by the hundreds in most courts. In a letter to me on Aug. 26, 1968, he wrote:

"I expect the police in Helena will continue to handle the intrusions on flower beds, broken taillights, curfew violation, fistfights, bicycle thefts, and the other minor offenses they regularly include in their annual report, without sending the offenders to me. I am not so concerned about these trivial matters."

Tough example set

Yet the majority of children in reform schools in every state in the nation are locked up for such offenses.

Judges across America cringe at the mention of Judge Loble. They are under public pressure due to the publicity given his "get-tough" recommendations.

Actually, Judge Loble jails few children. Nor does he publish names of most youngsters in trouble. He reserves this for those involved in extremely serious crimes.

Many judges oppose even this kind of publicity. They feel juvenile hearings should be closed to the public as a protection for the youngster. Yet, there is an argument for opening such trials: Often judges do things in secret they might not do if they were being watched by the public.

Take Albert, a bright, 13-year-old Negro. Twice he was locked up for shoplifting a few cents' worth of merchandise. The Nassau County, Florida, jail where he was placed was a filthy hole with heavy steel bars, steel bunks welded to the walls, and without an outside window in the cell. [It has since been cleaned up some.]

I checked at Albert's school. His principal, R. T. Anderson, was shocked when he learned the boy was twice jailed for weekends. Mr. Anderson said the boy was "not a troublemaker" and was an average student.

I visited Albert's home — a modest but clean dwelling being purchased by his parents. His father works the shrimp boats, and his mother sometimes does cooking. They have not been on welfare, she adds.

'Monument' builders help, too

Some judges are "monument" builders, yet do a great deal for children.

Take Judge Kenneth A. Turner in Memphis. He has a full-time public-relations man; a portrait of himself in the lobby; his picture in all juvenile-court offices; and even a photo of himself printed on interoffice memo pads. Some joke about his egotism. He says he "thinks" he once read something about the Gault decision, but he pays no attention to it.

Story of a "get tough" judge

What happens to a "get tough" judge when he has been in office for a while?

The Christian Science Monitor has followed the career of Milwaukee County Juvenile Judge George Bowman carefully for the past two years.

When he ran as a get-tough candidate two years ago he won easily — defeating an incumbent who was respected nationally.

Early in office Judge Bowman was quick to ship youngsters to a reform school — especially those who skipped school.

Even now he maintains a punitive image and has, as a result, strong support from such agencies as the Milwaukee Police Department.

But Judge Bowman says privately that he understands juvenile problems better now and is, in fact, far more compassionate than when he took the bench.

In 1968 he attended a summer seminar held in Boulder, Colo., by the National Council of Juvenile Court Judges. There he was exposed to views of social and behavioral scientists and leading judges.

He likes to talk of a philosophy learned there: "firm, prompt, certain treatment." By hard work and the help of a second judge he has cleaned up a serious backlog of cases.

Today, he says, more truants are "given an opportunity on probation" instead of being shipped off to reform school. Children in trouble are often assigned to special probation officers with low case loads — after a 30-day stay in the juvenile reform school that receives and studies delinquent children.

Several Wisconsin professionals who have watched Judge Bowman change were interviewed.

"He has seen that there are no simple answers," says one. "When he was campaigning for office, I think he honestly didn't know this. He thought if he had a tough image kids would stop breaking the law to avoid going to court.

"Now we see him groping for answers. The behavioral and social scientists in the community fought him from the start. This is unfortunate because Bowman, while he is hardheaded, has changed, and he could and would use their services.

"But they must remember that he is an astute politician and he believes he must continue to convey the tough image to retain the support of the police and the people.

"He has grown in his job, and it is time for the social and behavioral scientists to grow too."

Yet, he has written a handbook for juvenile judges in Tennessee; has efficiently organized his court; removed dependent and neglected children from the juvenile jail; built up a strong volunteer program; cracks down on fathers who skip children support payments; and has won the support of many in his community and state. In the past few years he has done more for children than most judges do in a lifetime.

In Denver, Judge Philip B. Gilliam has his portrait hanging in the detention home; has built himself—with taxpayers' funds—a posh, carpeted office complete with tiled shower. Yet out of his own pocket he has established "Judge Gilliam" trust funds to help children and has done much to improve detention-home conditions.

Most children in trouble come from multi-problem families. In some cases parents are involved in one court getting a divorce while a son or daughter is involved in a juvenile proceeding. (The breakup of a home often drives children to delinquent acts.) At the same time the family may be involved in a civil action because the parents have failed to pay their bills; perhaps the father has been arrested as a drunk.

While the people and problems are one, the courts handle them separately. The answer is to establish a true family court with a full range of services for the family. (Elsewhere on this page is a list of steps judges can take to improve juvenile justice.)

Too few judges do anything to force an improvement in the environment that has produced the delinquent child—even when there are laws on the books that would permit them to.

Some, like Judge Turner, are aggressive in finding foster homes, shelter care, halfway houses, and private institutions. In Boston, Judge Francis G. Poitrast, chief juvenile judge, finds almost any alternative to reform school:

"We pay $8,000 or $10,000, or $12,000 per child per year—whatever is needed to help that child," he says.

But few counties provide their judges with enough funds for adequate probation departments.

Special training available

Juvenile judges need special training. The Monitor sent a reporter to attend sessions of both the school run (last year in Boulder, Colo.) in Reno, Nev., by the National Council of Juvenile Court Judges, and the summer seminar at the University of Minnesota. The latter also accepts probation officers, policemen dealing with juveniles, and educators working with children in trouble.

Both are excellent and should be expanded. Similar training centers should be established in every region of the nation. State laws should make it mandatory for all juvenile judges to attend such a program at least a month before taking the bench.

Some argue that the juvenile courts are a fuzzy blending of the law, social work, psychiatry, psychology, and personal opinion. If a judge needs a master's degree in social work or psychology to do his job, as some maintain, then there are probably fewer than 100 judges in the United States who are qualified to hear juvenile cases.

Too often lack of knowledge results in abuses:

An alcoholic parent? Ship the child off to reform school. A mother who mistreats or ignores her children? Send the children away. A teacher who constantly ridicules a youngster until the youth finally swings on the teacher? Kick the child out of school; put him behind bars. A father who skips out on support payments, so his children are going hungry? Send the children to an inhuman institution.

This is happening in courts in all 50 states today.

The juvenile court was established roughly a century ago to protect children from adult criminal court. And yet this newspaper's study indicates that many hardened criminals are being better treated in court than are youngsters. Both society and the children are the losers.

CHAPTER IV

'Reach a child early enough'

Studies indicate more than half the youngsters in reform school
could better be helped at home under probation guidance.
Take a look at today's programs — why some fail,
why others are so successful in salvaging young lives.

I T WAS LATE THURSDAY WHEN MRS.
Lenore L. Williams, of Billings, Mont., got
the call.

A mother — a divorcee — was on the line.
She couldn't control her husky 13-year-old
son, Jerry, she said. When she told the boy
he had to be home by eight at night, he
used abusive language. Twice he knocked
her down. The mother wanted help.

Mrs. Williams is a probation officer in
Yellowstone County. She agreed to meet
Jerry's mother at 6:30 the following morning before the distraught woman went to
work.

They talked. After the mother left for
work, Albert Thomas, chief probation officer, picked up Jerry at home and took him
down to the office. Without a court hearing,
the boy was told to report to Mrs. Williams
once a week after school.

Tens of thousands of children in trouble
report to probation officers daily in the
United States. Thousands have had to go
to court. But thousands of others, like Jerry,
have not. They are known in the jargon of
probation as "informals."

Most correction officials believe that a
skilled probation officer with proper services available, and with adequate funds,
can do much to prevent delinquency. But
he must reach a child early enough — before he becomes entrenched in crime. This
study indicates that few courts have adequate probation programs. And few children receive attention until they are in
serious trouble.

Many programs 'too little, too late'

Traditional probation that offers too little,
too late is a waste of taxpayers' money. Such
programs do not change a child's way of
thinking and acting. They simply delay shipping him off to reform school — too often a
prison for children — to be punished. Reform

schools are filled with probation-department
failures.

Yet studies by the California Youth Authority show that well over half — perhaps
three-quarters — of those locked up might
be better helped at home. The percentage
of those who can be helped at home is even
higher in rural states such as Vermont,
Idaho, Iowa, New Mexico, and South Carolina.

This is all the more shocking when one
hears the words of George F. McGrath, the
highly respected head of the New York City
prison system, who holds that prisons and
reform schools cause crime:

"The public should be told that correctional agencies contribute enormously to the
crime rate," he said in an interview. "There
is a direct relationship between the growing
crime rate and our institutions.

"The people do not understand that. Public officials do not understand that. But it is
unquestionably true."

Mr. McGrath believes probation can help
solve the crime problem if the money is
available—along with qualified officers.

"You don't really have probation when the
officer is stuck with caseloads of 50 or 60 or
70 or 100 kids," he says. "All you can do is
paperwork. You're not counseling; you're
not getting kids back to school; you're not
getting them jobs. The success rate depends
on individual treatment. And trained
workers.

Many roles filled

"The public is being deceived because
they believe we have fancy programs. The
public is being misled because we only have
blueprints for programs, and the programs
are not being implemented."

Better probation is not the end-all answer
to delinquency, in that delinquency is so

deeply rooted in slum living, home and school problems, and a large variety of other societal flaws. It is not a quick panacea. But tied to other programs that deal with root causes, it plays a significant role. It can be of great value.

Probation originated in Massachusetts in 1887. The theory: Work with an individual before he is locked up and hopefully he will never need to go to prison.

What does a skilled probation officer do? If he does his job well, he helps fill in as a father to the child who has been damaged by a bitter divorce. He is the sounding board for frustrated youngsters who need someone to talk to. He is a kind of minister who, without preaching, helps the child with ethical and moral questions in a materialistic, uncaring age.

His job is to patch together fragmented families so that children can survive in their homes. He sees that a child gets proper dental and medical care. He makes sure youngsters have proper clothing for school.

He insists on special education for struggling children—finds a tutor when the school balks. He finds jobs for children when they have been stealing for food or pocket money. He takes deprived children on outings, helps them build a positive self-image to survive in an imperfect world.

In short, the ideal probation officer is a firm, steady counselor and the child's best friend. And he knows how to get things done.

But this isn't the case in most communities.

Probation too often is used as a threat to make a child behave. This is clearly the wrong approach, say such experts as C. Eliot Sands, Massachusetts commissioner of probation. For in time the threat wears off, and probably has not produced a meaningful change in a boy's way of thinking.

Officers often untrained

Probation officers are too often poorly paid, untrained workers, picked because they helped the judge in his campaign or because no one else wanted the job, or because the would-be worker decided he "wanted to do something about this delinquency thing." As one officer explained it in an interview, "It's tough, but it beats standing up all day on a factory production line."

This is unfortunate.

Probation plays a key role in what is sometimes called a mongrel system of juvenile justice—a system that is an uncertain mixture of law, social work, psychology, and personal opinion.

It can save taxpayers millions of dollars a year when it is effective.

A highly skilled probation officer is paid between $8,000 and $15,000 a year in the best states. He can work successfully and intensively with up to 30 children.

To lock 30 children for one year in a good institution—one capable of changing them from troublemakers to useful citizens —can cost taxpayers between $150,000 and $250,000. Yet many experts believe it is impossible for any institution to do as much for the child as the probation worker can. An institution can do little to change the environment that produced the delinquent. The best probation workers help rehabilitate whole families.

Stigma felt by many

Returning a child to the same environment that caused the delinquency destroys whatever good even the best reform school may have done, correction officials argue. That is one reason why so many children are recommitted to institutions, they add.

Children who go to reform schools face an added barrier: the stigma of being locked up.

Other parents warn their youngsters to stay away from the child who has been sent away. At school, teachers and student leaders may be cool or even hostile. Other youngsters may give the boy new status as a tough.

Whatever the reaction, the child in trouble is not a vegetable. He feels deeply. He may be emotionally immature. But this, according to the experts, may be because he has been deprived of the things all children need: love, attention, status, discipline— but not brutality. A few children in reform school have been spoiled by "doting parents," experts add. Such children run wild.

Some states see the light

It is essential to help children in trouble before they see themselves as criminals. Once this happens it becomes doubly hard to bring about change.

This is why, when parents are unable to bring about change, early and intensive probation is usually considered the best solution to the delinquency problem.

A few states have seen the light.

Since 1963, Ohio has encouraged counties to increase probation staffs (or hire their first probation officer) by offering matching funds for salaries. To qualify, a county must hire additional workers, using the 1959 staff size as the base.

Ohio has more going for it: The state also subsidizes schoolteachers who function as part-time probation officers. These teachers work with children in trouble in their own schools.

The state also pays up to $2 a day in matching funds for foster care of delinquent children without homes or those living in an environment that encourages delinquency.

George W. Jeffries, who heads the bureau of probation development for the Ohio Youth Commission, says 50 of the state's 88 counties participate.

Of the 30 who do not, Lucas County (Toledo) is the largest. There the probation staff has been cut since 1959.

Other counties have problems

A number of the other counties not in the program have delinquency problems. In the past fiscal year Wood County (Bowling Green) shipped 21 children to reform schools while 14 others were sent to the Ohio Youth Commission for evaluation and study. James Thompson, Wood County juvenile probation officer, has had a caseload of "around 180" youngsters. The court is now in the process of providing additional help.

Ross County (Chillicothe) committed 20 children to reform schools in the same period. Yet Ross County has only one part-time probation worker.

It seems certain that Ohio taxpayers would have saved money (not to mention children) if these youngsters could have been helped early by highly skilled probation workers.

But the counties are not totally at fault. Ohio has only come partway. Probation officers are subsidized only up to $2,400 a year, while the state will pay up to $3,000 for supervisors. Both figures should be doubled.

Ohio probation caseloads still run 50 or 60 or more children per worker. This should be cut even further. The state's taxpayers would still be money ahead.

California grew concerned over cramming children into institutions in 1965 when a record 6,174 were sent to the Youth Authority. The following year the State Legislature launched a probation-subsidy program. Counties are paid to keep troubled children at home.

After two full years of operation officials found 3,814 youngsters had been kept out of reform schools.

To have put these youngsters in institutions, California taxpayers would have paid out $15 million. The cost of the probation-subsidy program: $5.7 million—just over a third.

Recreation replaces counseling

Yuba County (Marysville) is one of the latest to sign up. Two new men have been hired. Each handles a caseload of no more than 25 boys and five adults. Next year a female officer will work with 25 girls and 5 women. Methods are improving, too.

The traditional probation officer sits in his office waiting for the probationers to file in for a few minutes' conversation.

Under the new Yuba County program, the two probation officers spend as much time as possible out of the office. Emphasis is on teaching by example rather than words.

The officers have taken two or three youngsters at a time into the mountains to ski. Or they may take several others on a weekend fishing trip. A ride to Sacramento for a concert or an evening at a pizza parlor, followed by a game of pool, can replace traditional counseling sessions. Summer camping is planned.

Children in trouble need strong, positive ties with adults, the experts explain. They need the guidance and help they haven't received at home because of parents who don't care or are too permissive or too rigid.

The program also includes what is known as "guided group interaction"—a cousin to group therapy used in mental hospitals. It is similar to the kind of give-and-take bull sessions found on college campuses. Two things are emphasized: self-knowledge and helping one another.

Yuba County's new program is a good example of what probation subsidy is all about.

To qualify, a California county must reduce a worker's caseload to 50 or less. The money is also used to provide "counseling, psychiatric treatment, and job counseling," says Allen F. Breed, director of the California Youth Authority.

But there is more. In four areas of the state experimental Youth Service Bureaus are being established. Yuba and neighboring Sutter County will open one of the four this summer.

Emphasis will be on preventing delinquency. Schools are being asked to find problem children and their families in the elementary grades. Then services of existing agencies will be offered: Boy Scouts, Campfire Girls, the Ministerial Association, credit counselors for families with money problems.

Parent education programs will also be taken to the neighborhoods—using churches and schools for meetings on why Johnny can't read or Billy throws stones at his sisters.

School grounds used

Lacking public transportation, the two counties have decided to bring recreation programs to the children, again utilizing schoolgrounds.

There are creative probation programs scattered across the United States. Minne-

apolis is noted for, among other things, its exciting probation-sponsored raft trips down the Mississippi River.

One of the best-known programs is the Citizenship Training Group in Boston—now in its thirty-third year.

Boys placed on probation attend a 12-week session for two hours every day after school. They are examined for physical, academic, and emotional problems, and take work-preference tests. Youngsters participate in both calisthenics and competitive games with staff members. The program also includes elementary handicrafts, working with leather and paper. And children are shown films and become involved in group discussions about their role and obligation as citizens.

But what of the typical probation officer?

This newspaper found that most are overworked and underpaid, and that few are aware of the exciting things happening in their field. It was found that most had never had training of any kind, nor had they read the best known probation books.

Even in Massachusetts, where probation was invented, problems exist. Until 18 months ago Albert J. Moquin had the help of only one woman to work with a caseload of over 300 in two cities—Fall River and New Bedford. This doesn't include the "informals"—those not found delinquent by the court.

"You see as many as you can as often as you can, but you can't do much," Mr. Moquin says. "And when one of us is on vacation or out for some other reason—well, you can guess what happens."

In November, 1967, a man was added to his staff. Last July another woman was hired. But the caseload has grown to over 400, plus "informals"—which means each staffer must work with 100 youngsters.

When children are in school, the time available for probation conferences is limited. Seeing 100 youngsters or even 60 or 70 every week—at least in a way that will alter delinquent behavior—is impossible. And one finds this is common in state after state.

Calvin Weldon, who works with delinquents for the New York Division for Youth near Syracuse was once a probation officer.

Alternative seen

"I've always felt that if there was just some way to keep these kids out of serious trouble for a couple of years they'd make it," he says. "A lot of the kids we put in an institution could be kept in the community if we only had the manpower to work with the family. All some of these kids need is somebody to sit down and listen."

Similar comments echoed across the nation.

What can one man in a rural community with little budget do? Plenty, if he has talent and imagination and likes children, say such experts as Paul Keve, who heads Minnesota's Department of Corrections.

The probation officer may be an outdoorsman. What better way to channel restless, troublesome children into wholesome activity while building a positive relationship? The probation officer may be a skilled auto mechanic who can work with boys who like cars. He may be able to teach them welding or some other masculine skill. Or his hobby may be golf, swimming, weight lifting, or archery.

Women can help girls on probation make clothing or cook. And vigorous sports like swimming and tennis should not be overlooked, experts add.

Michael G. Fleming of Livingston, Mont., proves what one probation officer can do. He has a bachelor's degree in business administration. He is a skilled magician and ran a magic shop for several years while working part time as a probation officer.

"I felt I was falling so short of what I thought could be done with kids that I asked to go on full time," he said. Two years ago he was paid $6,000 a year. His maximum salary will eventually be $9,000.

Every year he goes around to the schools and puts on a free magic show. He makes no pitch; just lets young people get to know him as a good guy.

He also has a radio show from 7:30 to 8 every Thursday evening. Sometimes he talks about the law, often he invites local youngsters to take part in a panel—usually without being identified. They discuss their views on drinking, haircuts, clothing styles, how to act on a date, or parent problems—basic questions that are too often ignored at home or at Sunday school.

Sometimes listeners call to discuss personal difficulties. Both teen-agers and Mr. Fleming may answer the questions. The program is well received by both young people and parents.

Once a serious family situation was helped when a boy blurted out that he hated to go home because his father was a drunk. The father was listening and was able to take the criticism and face up to his problem. He might never have listened in a direct confrontation.

Parents often drop in

Parents often visit Mr. Fleming's office in the courthouse basement to discuss their children. And youngsters with problems at home sometimes go to "Mike the Magic Man" instead of running away.

Probation officer counsels youths

He also writes a regular column, "Ask Mike," for the Livingston Enterprise, and covers subjects from curfew to use of BB guns to dropping out of school.

Unfortunately men like "Mike the Magic Man" are rare in probation. Too many lack skill and imagination. Instead they sit at their desks, hand out rules, and wait for children to break them.

In too many sections of the country there are no probation officers. This is the frustration of Judge Alan McPheron in Durant, Okla.

"I guess you might say I act as my own probation officer," he says. "I make it a practice to give the first offender a suspended sentence, and if he gets into trouble again, I send him up to the penitentiary.

"I've started accepting a plea of guilty and deferring the sentence six months. I check in the community to see how he's doing. If he's doing well, I defer the sentence another six months, and if he's still doing well, I withdraw the plea of guilty and enter a not-guilty plea."

Judge McPheron has been trying to establish a tax-exempt foundation to raise funds for a probation program. And he hopes some day to get community people to volunteer to help.

But now he has few alternatives. A youthful offender is sentenced to two years, then shipped off to the state prison for 60 days, with the other 22 months deferred.

Not everyone agrees that probation is worthwhile. Many policemen feel as Chief Howard J. Diehl, of Altamont, N.Y., does:

"The courts just slap their wrists," he said one fall night as we sat chatting in his patrol car. "Couple of weeks ago a 15-year-old stole two cars. He was already on probation for stealing one last year. His attorney pleaded him guilty, and the judge just put him back on probation.

"Last year kids put a lot of stuff on the railroad tracks—barbed wire, barrels, planks, things like that. We caught the kids —and they were just put on probation.

"We got narcotics around here. We arrested a 17-year-old who had some marijuana and some LSD when he was picked up. He was put on probation."

Crime increase cited

"Crime has increased tremendously around here—in our town [a suburb of Albany], it's gone up 21 percent, and 70 percent of those involved are under the age of 25."

Chief Diehl is a big man (6 feet, 5 inches), and he is respected by officers in neighboring towns. He works seven days a week, and is "on call constantly." There is little ques-

tion that he is dedicated. Or why he is frustrated.

But most corrections officials argue that the answer is not locking more youngsters up for longer periods of time. Rather it is in more effectively using probation and other correctional tools. This is as true in large cities as in rural areas.

This reporter found that in New York City, while there are some exceptional officers, the probation program is woefully inadequate. What worker, however skilled, can in a two-hour conference each month compete with the streets of Manhattan, Harlem, the Bronx, or Brooklyn?

Phoenix has the same problems as other cities. But it is trying to do something extra.

"Our community is concerned because so many kids believe they can commit a crime and get away with it," says Harvey Grady, rehabilitative program director for the juvenile court. "There are too many youngsters to give each one personal attention. Our court has 24,000 referrals a year.

"A youngster may be picked up in March for curfew. The police take him home. Two weeks later he's picked up for the same thing. This office [probation] may send out a letter to his parents. But he may be picked up for three or four curfew violations or several times for shoplifting without anything serious happening because of the lack of staff. So he feels he can get away with crime.

"We began STOP (Short-Term Orientation Program) on Oct. 2 to get at this. The parents bring the boy down in the morning. They are frightened, and they want to avoid court.

"We counsel them as a group. We tell the parents we want to give them immediate help. We ask them to voluntarily set up their own treatment plan in a written statement of specific guidelines to follow."

Emphasis is on making the parents responsible for preventing delinquency. This usually involves referral to a community agency that hopefully can help.

While it is too early to evaluate the plan, Phoenix officials call it "promising." One advantage, Mr. Grady says, is that under this program probation people are more likely to uncover "severe emotional disturbances, psychotic tendencies, or family disintegration." Such cases are then referred to appropriate community agencies.

Rules prepared

While some argue that a single morning session will not be enough, other professionals suggest that prolonged probation for a child also causes problems.

"For a juvenile a year seems like an

eternity," says Alfred Thorup of Carroll, Iowa. "There's such a thing as overkeep, and the youngster may give up if he doesn't get some time off."

For "not too serious a crime" he believes a child should be on probation "not less than three months and not more than six."

Most probation officers prepare written rules for youngsters—a point of debate today.

Mr. Thorup usually tells them not to ride in a car—except when driven by their parents or a school bus—for the first month. He will let them associate with youngsters only one year younger or older. He emphasizes church attendance. Except for older youths, they must attend school.

Many experts now argue that rigid rules are unrealistic. If the probation officer skulks around hoping to spot a violation, then he is playing a grim little "catch-me" game with the child. Finding ways to send a youngster off to reform school often becomes the goal.

Mr. Thorup's concern, like that of others in the field, is lack of alternatives. He would like a halfway house—a small group home for children who can't live with their parents or have no parents.

He tells of 13-year-old Tommy, whose father was "a drinker and a woman-chaser." When the home split up Tommy was sent to a church-run home for two years before being sent back to his mother.

Unfortunately, he preferred his father, whom he looked on as "seven feet tall." But his father didn't want him, nor would the church home take him back. He quickly got into trouble and at last check was in the reform school.

It is this kind of boy who could profit by a probation-run group home, Mr. Thorup explains.

Most probation officers also suggest foster homes are an answer. In a foster home one family cares for a child. The lack of one sent two Fremont, Neb., sisters to the reform school.

The girls' father has been a constant failure. The family has moved from one rented house to another. The father drinks heavily; the mother is an extremely poor housekeeper.

Both girls have run away—once in the family car. While probation didn't work, neither girl has committed serious crimes. Yet, for lack of a better place to send them, they were shipped to the reform school.

'Soft' probation hit

In hundreds of cities where police are dissatisfied with "soft" probation, or where no probation department exists, the police perform what is known as "station adjustment"—the child must report in regularly. Too few policemen are qualified to meet the needs of these children. It means police not only pick up youngsters, but also sit in judgment. The result is too often a kangaroo court.

Questions also must be asked about the use of "informal" probation.

"Where the behavior problem isn't serious we see it as unnecessary to take a youngster before a judge," explains Billings, Mont., Judge Ernest E. Fenton. "We would have to increase the number of juvenile judges to a terrific extent if we had to take every juvenile case to court."

Yet this writer found that a probation department can provide a direct route to the reform school. Thousands of children each year, on probation for minor offenses, are shipped off for breaking probation rules.

The best answer seems to be a separate agency—outside the police department or juvenile court—to deal with youngsters who have not committed crimes. This agency should be designed to help parents and children who come in voluntarily, as well as those referred for minor offenses by school officials and police.

Why does probation fail?

Why does probation fail? Kenneth Polk of the University of Oregon says that too often with probation "all we can offer is words," and children in trouble "need a lot more than that."

"You talk and then they go right back to the same old school, which is organized for the college-bound student, and to the same slum, the same parents, and all of the other things that have caused his delinquent behavior. What is accomplished?"

And yet Wilbur LaBorde, a New York City probation supervisor makes a strong case for the other side.

"When we talk with a child it may be the first time anyone has talked to him man-to-man—at least in terms of self-determination and his future."

James Lamb, who heads the Youth Development Center—a "reform school"—in Warrendale, Penn., points out that "you can't solve these problems by building institutions."

And J. D. Fleming, chief juvenile probation officer in Atlanta, who pessimistically notes that "some institutions are harming children less than others," steps out of the detention home and stares across at the city's $18 million stadium. Then he asks:

"We say our correctional system is weak because we lack funds; but is it possible that our society has become adept at hiding behind this excuse?"

CHAPTER V

'Too many of them get worse in our care'

This conclusion led one authority on juveniles to suggest
that for the most part it would be better for all concerned —
including society —"if young delinquents were not
detected, apprehended, or institutionalized." Too often reform
schools merely offer "advanced degrees" in criminality.
This chapter tells why.

ROBERT P. HEYNE OPENED HIS file drawer, pulled out a worn leather flogging strap, and held it up. It appeared to be at least two feet long; as broad as a man's hand; half as thick as a finger.

"Okay," he said. "You're right. We're using it again. We've got nothing to hide."

Floggings were common at the Indiana Boys' School until 1966. In that year Mr. Heyne's superior in Indianapolis announced the strap would be retired. The man who banned beatings was ousted when Gov. Edgar D. Whitcomb (R) took office a few months ago. The floggings quickly began again, although fewer children are being beaten than in the past.

Mr. Heyne says boys are strapped only five strokes on their bare buttocks. The floggings also are often tied to 30 days in solitary confinement.

Floggings described

A boy described his flogging to me. (This was later confirmed by a staff member.)

"They took me into the room where we watch TV. I was told to bend over the table. A security man held the strap. Mr. Heyne and some others stood around watching. They told me to drop my drawers. I kept looking around, and the security man slapped my face. Then he hit me with the strap. I went down to my knees. They pulled me up and hit me again. I went down to my knees. That happened five times. I couldn't sit down for three days. I couldn't lay on my back for a week until the welts went away."

Audie E. Langston, an employee of the Florida Division of Youth Services, witnessed past floggings at the Florida School for Boys in Marianna. He describes them as "sickening."

"A young boy [was] taken into a stark, bare, dimly lit room where he was compelled to lie on a small cot and receive licks with a heavy leather strap. At the time the strap was being wielded by a man who was at least 6 feet 3 inches and weighed well over 200 pounds. . . . The child quivers and writhes. . . ."

Robert M. Peterson, also an employee of the Florida Division of Youth Services, told of working at Marianna some 10 years ago. He recalled walking a child back from a flogging. The boy, he said, "was bleeding profusely."

The superintendent of the Marianna school recently was fired when he said publicly that he wanted to begin using the strap again. At last word he was fighting to be reinstated.

This newspaper's investigation into treatment of juveniles in 1969 found some experts comparing it to the handling of runaway slaves in the 18th and 19th centuries in the United States.

Punishments compared

Testimony of Pueblo crew members indicates they were treated little worse by their North Korean captors than are some inmates in the Indiana Boys' School, the Indiana Reformatory in Pendleton, the Arkansas prison system, the John G. Richard School in South Carolina, the Florida School for Boys, and other institutions across the United States.

Mr. Heyne's explanation for resuming

Society's dictum: Help youngsters in trouble—
but keep them out of sight

severe punishment at the Indiana Boys'
School: The runaway rate exploded from 79
in 1965 to 306 in 1966, and has been almost
that high since then. Runaways rile citizens
and government officials.

"The community and state have been on
our necks," he says.

Like juvenile judges who shake their heads
in despair because they see no alternative
to institutionalization, correctional officials
often feel forced to resort to corporal punishment when under public pressure. Indiana
is not alone in this.

Citizens of Marianna, Fla., became furious
when the runaway rate climbed after state
officials took away the strap. In states like
California, Ohio, and Illinois some institutions are surrounded by high fences.

Slapping was used to control boys in Delaware until this newspaper found five boys
with punctured eardrums. Officials have
complained that the runaway rate is up.
South Carolina officials also complain of
discipline problems now that beatings have
been abandoned after being exposed by this
newspaper.

Leaders in the correctional field say
flogging, slapping, and inhumane confinement *can* cut runaway rates. But this does
not resolve the basic reasons for runs:

Inadequate staff; far too little operational
money; institutions that are too large; the
mixing of tough hoodlums, emotionally disturbed youths, retarded youngsters, and
children who are largely dependent and
neglected; and a bankrupt rehabilitative
program.

"What is truly tragic is that the public
closes its eyes to the forces and lack of
resources within the institution which made
these youths want to flee," says Milton
Luger, president of the National Association
of State Juvenile Delinquency Program Administrators.

Focus criticized

"Futhermore, the public focuses upon its
short-range, immediate protection rather
than being concerned about the additional
hostility and hatred being engendered within
these youths as they are subjected to brutal-
ization to keep them confined."

Mr. Luger also has said that "with the
exception of a relatively few youths, it
[would be] better for all concerned if young
delinquents were not detected, apprehended,
or institutionalized. Too many of them get
worse in our care."

It is in keeping with the statement by
George F. McGrath, who heads the New
York City correctional system:

"Correctional agencies contribute enormously to the crime rate."

Or the comments of Oliver J. Keller, who

recently took over as head of the Florida
Division of Youth Services:

"We are working in a terribly primitive
field. Primitive. Punitive. Brutal. I don't
like large institutions. I don't like what
happens to children in them. One of my men
says living in a training school is as
cozy as living in a wash bay of a filling
station. I agree. The child is returned to the
streets with none of his family problems
solved. And he's more sophisticated in
crime."

Public goals conflict

All of this points to the core of the matter:
the public is poorly informed, and often
frightened. The result is two clearly conflicting goals:

The people and their elected representatives tell correctional officials to help these
youngsters — but keep them locked out of
sight. Don't take risks. Don't spend tax
money on foolish frills like strong programs
and skilled workers. Drab walls and tough
guards are enough.

In a report to a governor's study committee in Connecticut, Dr. Earl S. Patterson,
consulting psychiatrist to the Connecticut
School for Boys at Meriden wrote:

"[This] school has been a wastebasket,
and inevitably what is pitched into a wastebasket is thought of as waste. The boys are
in a program of criminality. The school may
be held responsible, but it is carrying out
the desire of the public, which, at the point
of commitment, is hostile and punitive toward the boy.

"The boy knows it and we know it, but
the public only knows, 'Get him away from
us, and don't bother us with the gory details.'
The net result of the way the school is being
used is that the state philosophy (which carries public approval) is in direct contradic-
tion to the actual policy (which follows
public demand)."

Reformatory visited

While the public is initially at fault, this
does not absolve institutional heads of blame
for stupidity, sadism, and neglect.

Take the Indiana Reformatory, a two-hour
drive east of the Indiana Boys' School.
Young men 15 to 30 are kept there.

Late last year Hershall Thomas took over
as superintendent after a series of riots and
other unbelievable events.

Gangs of tough prisoners roamed the cell
houses, forcing smaller boys to submit to
gang rape, he says. There were murders
and beatings.

I met one 19-year-old Negro youth from
Indianapolis whose face and chest was a
mass of ugly scar tissue. I was told another

inmate poured lighter fluid on him and set him afire while he slept.

I asked to visit one of the dungeons to talk to those locked up there. As the sergeant's key clicked in the lock in one of the heavy steel doors, I could hear rustling—like small animals scurrying from danger. Then the door swung open.

Blankets lacking

One young man, his eyes sunken in his hairy face, crawled toward the opening. The light made him blink like an owl. Another sat in the center of the cold cement floor hugging his knees. A third was on his haunches, leaning against the wall. The fourth was deep in the darkness.

There was nothing in the cell except a single toilet bowl. These four were not even given blankets. They huddled together to keep warm. Fed at 5 a.m. once daily, they had eaten only bread, gravy, and water the day I was there.

"Why are you here?" I asked one of them, a 27-year-old from Jeffersonville, Ind. "I witnessed a murder out there [in the cell house]," he said. "I asked to be put here because I wasn't safe. I been here 24 days."

The authorities confirmed this.

The other three also had asked to be locked up because they were terrified by conditions in the prison.

I turned to Sgt. O. F. Stoner, who was in charge at the moment, and asked why men who are placed in the dungeon for punishment got two meals and a blanket while these men got only one meal—the smallest of the day—and nothing to protect them from the cold, even at night.

"We try to discourage [voluntary] check-ins," he said. "We figure if we make it rough enough they'll go out and stay out. We don't want them in here."

Earlier I had asked Mr. Thomas about the younger boys — those 15 or 16 — sentenced there by judges.

"I hate to see them walk in the front door," he says. "They're not even really broken away from home yet.

"When a kid comes in that door he has no hope and he's feeling numb. We take his clothes away from him, put him in prison clothes, give him a close haircut, and he's no longer an individual.

"When the younger boys come in here they're easy prey for the older men. One inmate will protect a kid from other inmates, give him cigarettes, candy, and other commissary items, get him [obligated] until he can put enough pressure on the kid to get him involved in homosexuality.

"Rehabilitation? They get fed two stories here—our side and the older inmates' side.

We lose and the other side wins because we go home every evening. But the other side [the older inmates] are feeding them their story 24 hours a day."

Brutality persists

In most institutions some staff members are brutal—even when official policy is to dismiss staff members for striking youngsters.

Robert J. Harrington was brought in from Illinois to change the Maryland School for Boys. He battles brutality; he has suspended a number of staff members for striking children, fired others. Yet he admits it still goes on. And I found evidence of it there.

At the Stonewall Jackson School for Boys in North Carolina I was permitted to interview one articulate youth — an exceptional youngster in an experimental honor cottage. Officials chose him for the interview because, I was told, he was truthful. I asked him what he liked best about the cottage.

"You have more freedom over here, and they don't hit you in this cottage," he said.

In the Youth Development Center at Milledgeville, Ga., I asked the assistant superintendent to listen to two boys tell how one had been injured by a guard who hit boys in the forehead with the butt of a closed pocket knife concealed in his clenched fist.

Immediately following the incident both boys had been locked in solitary confinement cells so there was no possible chance of their getting together to cook up a story. Both told the same story separately, and the assistant superintendent did the questioning.

Yet the man seemed far more interested in putting the boys in their place for telling me about the situation than in getting at the truth. When I kept pressing him, he suggested that guards are too hard to find to make too much of the situation.

At New Hampton, N.Y., officials had complained to a superior when they learned that I wanted to interview youngsters—and with good reason.

"The kids will tell him we hit them," one New Hampton official said.

During one interview with several boys the youths were hesitant to talk about the way they were treated. Finally one youth got down on his stomach and peered under the closed door to see if anyone was listening. "They hit us," the boys said.

Deplorable conditions in Delaware and South Carolina have already been discussed in detail in earlier articles.

Many superintendents defensively lie about brutality. But not all of them do. Some are open and honest.

In Rhode Island, Superintendent Joseph

P. Devine has tried to eliminate staff brutality but says so far he has failed.

Corporal punishment is still authorized in Tennessee, Idaho, Montana, and other scattered states. Least evidence of physical brutality can be found on the West Coast, where more money is being spent on qualified staff.

Psychologists, psychiatrists, and others who work in the field say flogging or hitting children is only one form of brutality. Children in reform schools often are verbally abused by sarcasm, ridicule, and disdainful attitudes. Attempts to take away the child's individuality—so common in institutions—can be damaging.

So is the extreme use of solitary confinement (anyone who doubts this might ask someone to lock him in a closet for a few days).

I found hundreds of boys and girls around the nation locked in solitary-confinement cells for days, weeks, even months.

While some of the finest institutions for children in America can be found in the state of Washington, Green Hill (reform) School for Boys is a depressing institution.

Solitary confinement and maximum security is heavily used for minor offenses.

'Attitude' punished

Superintendent Robert D. Quant says, "Any person on the grounds has the right to place a boy in isolation for any reason, and he will stay there until the program committee meets." That can mean four days without review.

One boy was locked up for 15 days because custodial people felt he had a "bad attitude."

The maximum-security unit is a prisonlike structure with heavy iron bars on the cells. One boy had been held in a cell 2½ weeks for stealing cigarettes and raising a ruckus in his cottage. Another one got in a fight and broke a boy's nose. Others had run away.

In the Iowa Training School for Boys at Eldora, a riot in 1955 resulted in the construction of a bleak security unit. Boys peeked at me through small holes in steel doors. Reconstruction was under way when I was there last summer.

Glossary of juvenile terms

Commitment: In criminal court adults are *sentenced* to prison. In juvenile court youngsters are *committed* to institutions—often until age 21—a period sometimes longer than they might be sentenced to in criminal court for the same offense.

Probation: Instead of being committed, the child reports regularly to a probation officer in the local community. If the child breaks the law or probation rules he probably will be committed.

Detention home: Euphemism for children's jail. A secure institution used to store children for court.

Foster home: A long- or short-term family contract with the state or county to rear a child or children, but without adoption. State usually pays some basic expenses. Now being used for delinquents as well as dependent and neglected children in progressive regions.

Shelter care: Short-term care facility for dependent and neglected children who cannot stay in their own homes for a variety of reasons.

Reform school: An institution where youngsters aged 7 to 21 (varies with state) are stored up to a year or more. Also called

training school, boys' school and girls' school, state home, youth development center, welfare home.

Reformatory: Prison for older offenders, usually between ages 15 and 21, sometimes up to 30.

Diagnostic and reception center: A fairly new kind of institution where children are tested by professionals before being sent to reform school, reformatory, or other institution.

Aftercare: Euphemism for parole. Implies (but does not always include) skilled supervision and help for the child after release from an institution.

Group home: A home for boys or girls who cannot live with their parents for a variety of reasons. An alternative to institutionalization. Size may vary from 4 to more than 30 children. Children live, go to school, and work in community. Professionals may run "treatment programs" as part of group-home living.

Halfway house: A group home. More accurately a home halfway between reform school or reformatory and the child's own home. Helps bridge gap between institutional living and open society.

Youths march to lunch

In most reform schools emphasis is really not on solving a child's problems or on helping him reenter the community as a useful citizen. Rather a little game is played. The rules vary, but the key is whether the child "adjusts" well to institutional life. This, even though institutional living has little to do with survival in a poor home or in the streets of Harlem, Chicago's West side, or in rural slums.

Even in the institutions using a "reward" system (rather than punishment) the payoff is for conformity.

Dr. Patterson explains how this works at the Connecticut School for Boys. While his report was written about the school in 1967, it is still accurate, he says. And this writer found it could apply to most reform schools for boys or for girls in the United States.

"At present boys admitted to the school are expected [by the staff] to reach a high level of conformity to [the institution's] pattern of procedures. Delay by the boy in doing so will bring punitive action against him in increasingly severe types, delay in classmanship advance [a system of rewards], physical punishment, isolation. Continuing failure to conform will produce continuous isolation and finally release or, in the past, transfer to another institution."

"A boy who conforms . . . will soon be labeled as changed, adjusted, or improved . . ." even when the conformity is a sham.

Basis questioned

Dr. Patterson adds that some boys who refuse to conform are given a "superior" rating and released just to get them out of the institution. In other instances staff will "bend the rules to create special privilege in order to win the boy over to an *appearance* of conformity."

What do boys who either conform or pretend to conform learn from this? Dr. Patterson answers with six points:

1. Lying, dissimulation, and pretense in order to placate persons in positions of strength. This implies no need or intent to change and denies personal responsibility for behavior.

2. The usefulness of power over weaker persons to control them or force them to certain ends.

3. The legitimacy of physical assault in order to effect goals.

4. Use of ridicule and humiliation to control a psychologically weaker opponent.

5. Rules are made to be bent—if not broken. The only ethic that truly applies is "don't get caught."

6. Hypocritical subterfuge to make an apparent attainment of a goal. What is real

is what people can be fooled into accepting. "Saying will make it so."

It is clear that children understand the institutional game. Dozens of youths interviewed told me they were just "doing time," and that if they followed the rules they would do "easy time."

In the Los Guilucos School for Girls in California I found a Negro girl from a terribly deprived home who refused to conform. She had been locked in her room four days for this and for losing her room key.

I questioned the psychologist who had her locked up. The woman not only admitted that the girl "probably should never have been sent here in the first place," but added that she herself might rebel if forced to conform to a group in a closed institution.

Girls are usually better treated than boys for a variety of reasons. This is partly because women run the institutions. But largely it is because most girls are locked up, not because they have snatched purses or stolen cars, but rather because they have run from intolerable homes or have become sexually involved with men at an age considered to be too young by society.

Offenses restricted

Miss Regina Flynn, superintendent of the New Jersey State Home for Girls, puts it this way:

"Girls, unlike boys, offend more against themselves than against other persons and property. Their offenses are usually first noted by schools in the form of truancy, then staying out late, running away from home, and involvement with boys."

Miss Ward E. Murphy, who runs the girls' school and women's prison in Maine (and worked in Virginia prior to that) estimates that "not more than 10 percent are criminals."

Take Sally, a Maine girl. Her mother traveled and had several children by different men.

Sally was given to her mother's sister — a home where both husband and wife were constantly drunk and Sally was mistreated. Sally kept running away.

On April 5, 1961, she was sent to a private school for emotionally disturbed children. On July 1, 1962, that institution decided treatment was not successful. So she was sent to a psychiatric hospital. After five months she was discharged and turned over to the welfare department. On that same day she was sent to Stevens Training Center, a reform school for girls.

Officials say there was no other place for her to go.

At the reform school she was "rude, impudent, defiant." She ran away 14 times.

Then on Dec. 4, 1963, she was sent to the reformatory for women — although Sally had *never* committed a crime.

Sally's experience is too often typical of the process by which society helps make criminals. Fortunately, in her case the reformatory had something which most lack: a halfway house on the grounds.

Sally entered the local public school where she completed 8th, 9th, and 10th grades. During the summer she worked at resorts. She dated a boy—a high-school graduate—for a year. When he completed two years in the Army they were married and now have a baby.

It became clear as I visited this nation's reform schools that not only is rebellion against regimentation normal—especially for a child who has been fighting for survival for 10 or 12 years—but also that running away from these institutions is normal.

Running away explained

Children in trouble often are compared to dogs that have been kicked and beaten. They trust no one, and when someone raises a hand they either cower in a corner, fight back, or slink away.

This helps explain the runaway problem. Some children have been running away from unpleasant experiences or pressure all of their lives. This is the way they react when threatened.

This is true of both girls and weaker boys.

It was shocking to discover that most youngsters locked in solitary confinement are not the assaultive brutes. Instead they are the weak ones who have either run from the homosexuality found in these institutions, from assaultive staff members and inmates, or have become so homesick they cannot stand it. (Almost every runaway from a training school heads for his home.)

Yet those who run the institutions seem not to recognize this. Officials continue to flog these frightened children or lock them in solitary confinement, while the rough are rewarded because they "conform."

As one tours correctional institutions it becomes clear that few administrators are imaginative people. Mr. Luger lays this in part to the public, which only asks that children in trouble be kept out of sight.

"Why then should program administrators seek to be creative?" he asked sadly, when he testified in Washington recently. "Why should they not settle for custody and control instead of treatment? Why then should not the goal of institutions be a trouble-free tour of duty rather than true attitudinal change on the part of young offenders?"

But this is only part of the answer. Working in a correctional institution gives one little status, and in fact may result in being looked down upon. Pay is extremely low. Institutions often are located in rural areas where bright college graduates find life dull. Dealing with the dregs of society is not pleasant work.

Fund lack criticized

"What multimillion industry could survive in a competitive market with executives paid the salaries of training school superintendents (from $5,000 to $15,000) and without sufficient funds for research to improve their product, eliminate inefficiency in production, and to seek new facilities for more acceptable products?" asks Sherwood Norman, director of Youth Correction Services for the National Council on Crime and Delinquency.

Homosexuality is often a problem at training schools, but one finds it most prevalent at girls' schools—though the girls usually revert to normal activity once they are returned to mixed society.

The most blatant example was found at the Bon Air School for Girls in Virginia. There large Negro and small white girls walked, arms entwined, across the campus —the Negro girls playing the male role, the white girls the female.

The problem is common from Massachusetts to California, and in some schools stronger girls are very aggressive.

In New Jersey and in other states girls developed "phantom families" with one playing the mother, another the father, while others were children, aunts, uncles, and cousins. Many have been rejected by their own families.

Girls schools also are sometimes so protective that they may never help inmates come to grips with their basic problem— a craving for parental love that they have never felt. This often results in promiscuity, according to those working with delinquent girls.

Interviews with both girls and staff at the Gainsville School for Girls in Texas and at the State Home and Industrial School for Girls in North Carolina indicated that the girls are never given a chance to face up to their problem.

Those working in other girls schools asked how—when a girl is locked up for being promiscuous—this problem can be resolved if it is never discussed with them by their counselors or in group meetings.

Rooms crowded

One of the worst weaknesses of institutions is lack of activity for active children. The night I visited the Ferris School in Delaware one staff member was absent and two cottages were combined with only one man to supervise. Boys were crowded into two noisy rooms with little to do.

In South Carolina boys went to their crowded dormitories and sat on their beds in their underwear after supper.

In Indiana teen-age boys were put to bed at 8 p.m. because of lack of staff. There is an inoperative swimming pool on the grounds and a gym. Staff members take boys out to play for short periods after supper "when they are in the mood." For some guards this means once every week at best.

I was urged not to visit the Indiana Boys' School on Good Friday because employees get the day off and the institution is "shut down." That means a skeleton crew and no program.

Even at Maple Lane in Washington, one of the nation's finest reform schools, there is little activity on a Sunday afternoon. The Sunday I visited Maple Lane I found girls deeply depressed because they had no visitors.

Visiting limited

In every training school I toured, I was told weekends are the worst. This is partly because of 19-century visiting practices.

In North Carolina, for example, the rules read: "Each student is entitled to one three-hour visit per month by members of his or her immediate family after a 30-day orientation period in the school."

Young men at the State Correctional Institution at Camp Hill, Pa., are allowed two hours of visiting per month.

The visiting privilege is withdrawn in most institutions if the youngster's behavior is poor.

And yet in more progressive systems officials say they permit visiting as often as the parent will come and they also encourage social workers to hold conferences with both parents and child present so that they may help uncover conflicts that hinder rehabilitation.

In the past, boys with a variety of problems were thrown together, all to be treated in the same manner. This is changing. The trend today is toward careful, individualized diagnosis of problems by trained professionals. Unfortunately, this is not always coupled with a meaningful program.

In Illinois the Diagnostic and Reception Center for Boys has a liberal visiting policy, and the diagnostic staff is often praised.

Twenty of the 200 youngsters being held are getting a little help from some very skilled nuns who teach in nearby schools. And there is an effort being made to get more volunteer programs going.

But 90 percent of the boys are held in sterile tile rooms. There they sit for weeks playing cards or staring at television while a guard leans against a wall or sits with his feet up on a chair.

What normal, sane mother would lock her children and 15 or 20 neighborhood youngsters in a room for hours week after week with nothing to do?

The smaller youngsters do go to an art-and-crafts room, but only once or twice a week. Discussion groups are held for only an hour or so weekly.

What the boys most need is help in learning to read and in developing improved attitudes. Yet, too much of their time is taken up with "busywork" — like making beds and polishing floors till they glisten.

When I asked why the present custodial staff couldn't do more than lean against the wall, watching the kids—or at best occasionally playing Ping-pong or cards with inmates—I was told that they either were not qualified or not interested.

Changes indicated

And yet I did meet one guard, Bennie Thompson, who was being constructive. He was teaching children to read, to spell, to grow plants in a tin can. He had to bring in his own materials, paid for out of his own pocket. But he was doing it. Other guards opposed him.

When I asked Charles Handley, the institution's bright young superintendent, why the children had no reading material, he said it was available—there was a library—the children just weren't interested. I asked to see the library.

It was a small room, an office in regular use. Behind the door was a bookcase with some torn books, year-old Reader's Digests, a few Better Homes and Gardens, an old Saturday Evening Post, five or six comic books, and some other magazines with the covers torn off.

It is doubtful that even normal youngsters would find these ragged adult magazines interesting.

Fortunately, Mr. Handley, who was defensive at first, reversed himself a few days later and indicated changes would be made.

But in looking at correctional institutions one always comes back to the American people and their elected representatives.

As the National Council on Crime and Delinquency's Mr. Norman points out:

"With the rise of delinquency statistics and increasing demands to relieve overcrowding in detention homes and training schools, busy legislators give way to the easiest 'solution' to the problem—build more and larger institutions.

"It should be obvious that if more effective community-based treatment is made available, fewer youngsters will be committed to the state. In spite of these facts, the major trend is the perpetuation of the correctional rut we are in.

"Legislators are seldom aware that large institutions actually contribute to delinquency."

Troubled youngsters may find communication almost impossible

CHAPTER VI

'Bulldoze them to the ground'

That's the advice many concerned correctional authorities offer.
For little reforming goes on at these children's prisons.
Too many are staffed with "emotional rejects" who themselves
have failed to adjust to society. The "treatment" such
workers mete out often further warps already
troubled young lives.

O NE NEVER KNOWS WHAT HE WILL find hidden behind a locked reform-school door.

At the Florida School for Boys at Marianna I found Jim, a frail 16-year-old. His pajamas were covered with blood. In his hand he held a glass diffuser pried from a recessed lighting fixture. Jim had used it to gash his arm a dozen times from wrist to elbow.

No one seemed to care.

The night before, while in a large day room supervised by two guards, he had eaten a light bulb. No one seemed to care about that either.

As punishment he had been locked in solitary confinement — a common practice in institutions with neither qualified staff nor facilities to handle emotionally disturbed children.

Series of foster homes

Jim's life has been filled with people who seem not to care. He has a "bunch" of step brothers and sisters he has never met, the result of his mother's living with various men. Welfare officials labeled him neglected, and the court placed him in a series of foster homes. He always ran away.

He was first sent to Marianna at age 12 and was held two years and two months. During that time he was hit by guards and was twice beaten with a flogging strap, once for fighting with a larger boy who was trying to force him into a homosexual act.

After living in a foster home for a year and a half, he was returned to Marianna for running away from another foster home and for sniffing glue. Jim had been locked up the second time for more than a year when I met him. He now was being punished for sniffing gasoline fumes at the school.

Much of reform school "teaching" goes on away from the classroom

After a lengthy interview I asked a school official to talk to Jim. Suddenly the boy began to shake, tears poured down his face, and he talked compulsively.

"My whole life I've been slapped and kicked and beat," he said. "When things get too bad, I run. I just kept runnin' and runnin' and runnin'. I never broke into a place—I was too scared. I never stole a car —I don't even know how to drive."

He talked for nearly half an hour. When he stopped he seemed less tense. As he was led back to his cell the program director turned to me and said with no little surprise:

"This is the first time that boy has ever opened up."

It was not the only time that happened as I toured the nation's reform schools. Too often staff members have no time to talk to children. Many youngsters are reluctant to discuss delicate matters with officials who can punish them or prolong their stay. Some workers believe they are paid to be guards—nothing more, nothing less.

At the Gainsville School for Girls in Texas one official said staff members are under orders to talk only of trivial things.

Many employees are thrown into battle without training.

Cruelty of indifference

I watched a very unpleasant young guard order small children around at the Fairfield School for Boys in Lancaster, Ohio. He was disciplining some by having them stand with their noses pressed against lockers for long periods. When I asked Morris J. McCoy, deputy superintendent, about this he said the guard was new and that he had never seen him before.

Not that staff or administrator can be totally blamed. Some who become involved with these children find themselves emotionally exhausted. Normal middle-class teen-agers in an average home can be trying at times. And one underpaid worker assigned to 20 or 30 or 50 or more children in trouble obviously cannot find time to listen to each child at length.

Yet too often workers are indifferent. Jim's case was a typical example.

The school nurse didn't learn that Jim had eaten a light bulb until I told her 24 hours later. And I was the one who informed her of the cuts on his arm. No one else bothered to tell her. Even then she was not permitted to see the boy.

A guard was supposed to check on Jim and the other boys locked in solitary on the far side of the building every half hour. To prove he made his rounds the guard was to write down what each child was doing.

In talking to a conscientious night man — a new guard — I discovered that he was under orders from his superior to fake the report. The boys had never been checked during his eight-hour shift for the several months he had been there.

Faking reports in reform schools is not unusual. Nor is negligence of duty.

At the Indiana Boys' School, for example, men working as social workers (most are social workers in name only and are not really qualified) were to check on boys in solitary confinement daily. An official there seemed surprised when I told him boys were fortunate if they saw their social worker once a week. He said he would try to change that.

Too often administrators fail to understand their goal is to help children in trouble. Like inmates who stay too long, officials become "institutionalized." They believe smooth operation and staff comfort are ends in themselves. This is the case in Delaware, where officials are more concerned with staff morale than boys with punctured eardrums.

Even when administrators understand their goal, few can reach them. Some lack leadership ability.

Staffing problems observed

Guards—sometimes men who barely read and write—"run" institutions by banding together and threatening to quit. In rural areas the pressure can be great because cousins, aunts, uncles, and neighbors are hired.

Robert T. Grey, superintendent at the Connecticut Reformatory in Cheshire, complained that some staff members "are harder to handle than the inmates."

If there is one common cause of frustra-tion at training schools it is staff. Leaders in the field agree that guards or cottage parents spend the most time with children and thus are the most influential people in the institution.

"I'm sick and tired of getting nothing but emotional rejects," says Joseph P. Devine, the exasperated superintendent of the Rhode Island Training School for Boys.

"What do you expect to get when you pay $3,100 a year for a 60-hour work week?" asks a South Carolina official explaining deplorable conditions in reform schools there.

"We don't have standards for staff. All we get is a warm body," says Francis A. Ordway, superintendent of the Lyman School for Boys in Westboro, Mass.

"Male cottage parents start at $86 a week and females get even less. Sometimes the boys [when parolled] can make more money than that.

"The boys we get have failed in society. But the people we hire have too. All we get are the leavings. Oh, we have some good staff, but that's not because of something we've done."

At the Fairfield School for Boys in Lancaster, Ohio, guards — the staff members who spend the most time with the children —are required to have only a 10th grade education. They start at $96 a week and in 18 years can work up to $129.

There are fringe benefits at Fairfield. Children provide a form of slave labor for staff. Youngsters in the auto shop, for example, work on an employee's car for 50 cents an hour. Of this, 25 cents goes to the boy's account and 25 cents goes into the school-entertainment fund.

Work and punishment

Youngsters also spend considerable time running a farm to supply fruit and vegetables for their school and other institutions. They operate the laundry and do other menial tasks—a common institutional practice.

There is controversy on this point. For while on the surface letting children work saves taxpayers money and may be good for the children, many experts ask if this is sufficient to bring about a meaningful change in a child's behavior.

If youngsters hoeing weeds fail to gain a better self-image and then graduate from the reform school into more serious crime —and thousands do—then a few dollars saved on vegetables can be costly. And giving children farm work is often the only effort made to rehabilitate them.

For a youngster locked up, the break provided by farm work does have therapeutic values but accomplishes little in the way of changed attitudes.

At the Youth Development Center at Warrendale, Pa., one of the state's more forward-looking institutions, farming was discontinued by Superintendent James Lamb because he does not believe it helps them resolve deep-seated problems.

At the Iowa Training School for Boys, Anthony P. Travisono, superintendent at the time of my visit but now in Rhode Island, said, "We sold the farmland three years ago. We get very few farm kids, and we don't see much value in storing kids on a big farm."

Dale E. Swenson is superintendent of Echo Glenn Children's Center in the mountains above Seattle, one of the nation's finest training schools. Mr. Swenson opposes use of children as institutional maintenance workers.

"Take these kids off work details in most institutions and the institution would collapse," he says. "Work is valuable only as a learning experience."

What are children learning? Take the Youth Training Center in St. Anthony, Idaho. Classroom teachers and other staff members stuff them with stories about how work is virtuous. But when they misbehave, the youngsters are assigned to work crews as punishment.

Other experts add that perhaps farm work was meaningful 30 years ago because reform school graduates might find farm work after release.

Learning and earning

Some, like Mrs. Elizabeth Bode Van Waters, superintendent of the Massachusetts Industrial School for Girls at Lancaster, take the opposite view. She says, "I have a thing about farming, about the feel of the good earth." Her girls farm because she believes it is a "healthy, productive, fundamental occupation."

Some institutions consider work as job training. At the Illinois State Training School for Girls at Geneva, inmates who work in the laundry may live on the grounds and work in laundries in town, although at reduced wages.

At New Hampton, N.Y., several boys have been taught to weld. They earn $100 a week in town while living at the training school. The program is new.

The controversy over children farming, learning a trade, and over corporal punishment and solitary confinement, as discussed in earlier articles, indicates the confusion found in the juvenile field.

Everyone—layman or professional—has a theory. But in a field as barren of research

and as complex as this one, no philosophy has won out. Treatment methods change as often as hair styles.

There are some basic standards. Corporal punishment is generally abhorred by leaders in the correctional field.

Federal funds used

The majority of reform schools have—in recent months—used federal funds under Title 1 of the Education Act of 1965 to set up elaborately equipped reading laboratories.

Many try to help boys and girls learn a trade or skill. Most turn out short-order cooks, welders, auto repairmen, printers, butchers, or lawn-maintenance workers. In some institutions, older youngsters may, if they stay long enough, earn state certification as barbers and beauticians.

In many schools the superintendent defends his current program—often a combination of work, schooling, and discipline —as "the answer." He points to whatever yardstick he can grasp as "proof." Often he will criticize the programs of other reform schools.

Conflict over which "panacea" is best has been going on for years. This, according to Allen F. Breed, head of the California Youth Authority, develops when various professions "come into vogue," pushing other disciplines aside.

"One can recall that time which might best be described as the *moral training period* when the idea of discipline and repressive confinement was thought to enhance personal controls," he says.

"Then there was the *vocational training period* when institutions developed their entire program around the concept that by teaching a youth the skills of an occupation he could be released to find his rightful place in industry and again be accepted into community life.

"We also had the *recreational period* when playground directors told us to teach a boy how to play and you have taught him how to live with his fellow man.

"About that time the 'life can be beautiful' era came into bloom and its advocates preached the *relaxed permissive atmosphere* and the idea that a happy child is a well-adjusted child.

"Academicians pushed their way into the scene claiming that *school achievement* governed the social adjustment and the panacea could be reached by teaching delinquents to read better.

"Next we had the *period of diagnosis* and the social scientists came out of the ivy-covered halls of learning and left their parlor games of testing to become our messiahs of methodology to determine why Johnnie acts the way he does.

"More recently, the good doctors from Topeka, Vienna, and points east came forth to lead us into the *psychiatric period,* in which we thought of our clients as sick people in need of medically oriented care.

"This has been followed with the *therapeutic community,* which in the broadest sense of the term incorporates all of the disciplines and all of the members of the institution community—staff and inmates—in the treatment process."

This last point involves a team approach —social workers, psychiatrists, guards, schoolteachers working together. But does this happen? No, says Mr. Breed, because workers do not share a common goal.

"Most of our supervisors [guards] see their jobs as controlling inmates and preventing serious problems from occurring.

"Most of our teachers see their jobs as producing academic or vocational growth.

"Most of our counselors see their jobs as processing the necessary paperwork and 'counseling' boys around major problem areas that may occur.

Basic causes untouched

"Maintenance, feeding, farm and other service personnel see their jobs as meeting the production demands of the institution." None of these activities are the primary goal, he says.

"We must recognize that the basic goal of all of us should be to change delinquents into nondelinquents."

Until staffs recognize this and work as treatment teams with common goals "treatment will not take place," he adds.

But even this may not be the answer if large institutions are, in fact, poor places to help children.

As has been stressed in this series, institutions fail, in part, because they cannot deal with the basic causes of delinquency.

What can a reform school do about an alcoholic home? Poverty? The breakdown of the family? High mobility that gives children few roots? The failure of the church to meet the challenge of an age that worships money, cars, big houses, clothing, toys, and other goods? The pursuit of pleasure as a national pastime? The trend to escape in drugs, alcohol, even television? The withering of the tradition of helping one's neighbor?

Attention-seeking is common

Most children in trouble read at a level at least three years below other children of the same age. Some cannot read at all.

Most have a strong dislike for school. Some are mentally retarded. Others are hyperactive. Some are emotionally ill. While boys are generally normal in appearance, although some may be small for their age, a high percentage of the girls can be described as very plain or overweight. Many children in trouble are immature and extremely selfish.

Bed wetting is fairly common—even for tough city youngsters 14 or 15 or 16. Some teen-age girls still suck their thumbs. Many have dental problems. Girls usually have been sexually active. Both boys and girls are usually starved for affection and attention.

Permanent homemade tatoos often are applied with needle, thread, and ink or with a ball point pen while in a detention home, jail, or reform school. Other youngsters have ugly scars. To prove their courage some placed lighted cigarettes on their arms.

Few children in trouble ever have succeeded at anything except irritating parents, teachers, neighbors, policemen—most adults they come in contact with. They do not make their school ball teams; they do not make high grades. Often they have not had an opportunity to earn money with a part-time job—although many are excited about the prospect of working.

A reform school only emphasizes these failures and makes it more difficult to help the child.

"When you take the child from his parents—from his home and neighborhood, the court and community is telling the child 'we don't want you—we don't need you,'" explains Washington State's Mr. Swenson.

"You put the child in an environment of tainted people with no positive models except the keepers — men and women who may themselves be distorted within — and then call that corrective."

Reform-school administrators too often lack alternatives. They have a school and/or work program, and if this doesn't fit the child's needs that is too bad.

It is like having only one shoe store in town, and that store carries only one size of shoe — seven-A. Everyone in need of shoes must wear that size regardless of what they need.

Special cases noted

A reform school may be prepared to deal with Billy, a 14-year-old with reading problems who comes from a poor home and was caught breaking into a filling station, or Sharon, a bright girl who runs away from home. But what will they do with:

Debbie, a huge, poorly coordinated 12-year-old Galveston, Texas, girl with an IQ of about 60, who sometimes sees birds flying out of walls.

Sandra, a 15-year-old Washington girl who, after being sexually used by her father since she was 11, developed homosexual tendencies and is a prostitute because she "likes the money," and has not been in school in two years.

Carl, a 7-year-old California boy who compulsively lights fires and burned down a neighbor's house.

Beth, a bright, 16-year-old middle-class girl from Salt Lake City who started taking LSD and ended up leaving home.

Harold, 15, who has never broken the law but has been in Massachusetts reform school three years because his father has disappeared, his mother doesn't want him, and the judge decided there was nowhere else to send him.

These are all real cases. The Texas girl might be sent to a special school for retarded children in Denton. But she is 80th on the list, officials say. The child who is No. 1 on the list has been on that list two years, they add.

This problem is typical nationally. In Illinois, for example, one official estimates some 2,000 to 3,000 retarded children are waiting to enter institutions.

The emotionally disturbed child often has nowhere else to go. Few mental hospitals are prepared to help youngsters. Many have become dumping grounds for unwanted children.

Suggestions for improvement

At Logansport, Ind., a children's unit was recently established. Of the 50 children there only a handful were really different from those found in a typical reform school, orphanage, home for dependent and neglected children, or school for retarded children.

It is easy to lock up these children. But if they are to be salvaged then they must be able to return to the community.

Recognition of this has led thoughtful men and women dealing with children in trouble to urge redoubling of efforts to help children in their home communities. In line with this, John A. Troike of the Illinois Youth Commission suggested that the best answer to the reform-school problem is to "bulldoze them to the ground."

So far no legislature has had the courage to follow this advice—even when men like Washington State's Mr. Swenson say with conviction:

"The institution is the worst form of treatment there is."

Assuming that reform schools, prisons, and other institutions for children remain in use, then the stopgap answer must be the improvement of these institutions.

Physical plants are poor in much of the East and Midwest. In some sections of the South and most of the Far West they are better.

But an institution cannot be measured by its buildings. As in a university, the key is the staff.

The public must see that institutions are headed by the best possible people; that they are kept small—50 is often considered the ideal size; that they are designed to help a variety of children with a variety of problems; that workers are intelligent, compassionate, skilled people.

Mr. Breed, of California, sees two advantages of holding children in institutions. This "guarantees their attendance" in programs and makes it possible to coordinate services of a variety of professionals.

But first the institutions must find qualified professionals, and those in institutions must be backed up with help in the home communities.

Administrators constantly complain that the psychologists and social workers they hire "have more problems than the kids."

Information lacking

But the social workers and psychologists complain too. Many deal with 100 children or more. Often they have little or no background information on the children.

"We're supposed to have field workers who send us information about the child and his family," says a social worker at the New York State Training School for Girls. "I've had kids here for three months without any data. And even those who call on the homes aren't doing their jobs. They tell us how many other kids in the family and whether the home is clean or dirty—things like that. But they don't send us information that means anything. And they're not helping parents.

"Last Sunday there was a woman up here who said, 'Hey, I thought somebody was supposed to tell me how to help my daughter.'"

Usually the community court is supposed to supply training schools with a report.

Says one official at the Iowa Training School for Boys in Eldora: "We're supposed to get reports from the county that sends the boy, but frequently we don't get anything."

Shortage of professional staff can be readily seen at State Correctional Institution at Camp Hill, Pa. The day I visited last summer there were roughly 800 boys between the ages of 15 and 21. Because it was summer the number was down.

The staff consisted of 140 guards, 1 psychiatrist, 4 psychologists, and 4 social workers.

While the Boys School at Green Hill, Wash., can pay a better salary than most institutions, and its table of organization calls for eight psychiatric social workers, it has only two who are actually qualified.

Not only does staff have to be adequate, but there are other considerations. One is extremely simple but is consistently overlooked. Staff and children must be matched. This is true not only of social workers and guards but of parents, schoolteachers, and all others who come in contact with children.

Maturity scale developed

Dr. Rita Q. Warren, a social researcher with the California Youth Authority, has developed a scale ranging from one to seven to measure the social maturity of children—making matching easier. It is based on one's relationship to others or "I-level" (for interpersonal relationships).

Lowest on the scale: the infant who is totally dependent and self-centered and who knows only that when he cries he gets help. Next the child who recognizes a basic relationship between himself and another human.

And so on up to the opposite end of the scale to the individual who has great insight into his own behavior and the motivation and behavior of others. The "six or seven" is a rare individual who is aware of the many roles he and others play day by day and is not self-centered.

Individual staff members are measured for their strengths and to discover which kinds of children they work best with. Some are tolerant of the extremely immature child, but do not work well with the sophisticated delinquent. Others may not be able to stand the hyperactive child, but are very patient with plodders.

Most delinquents fall into the two, three, or four category, while workers tend to be fours, fives, and occasionally sixes.

Too few correctional workers—even the trained professionals—really understand the children they deal with.

In a booklet published by the Office of Juvenile Delinquency and Youth Development, a division of the U.S. Department of Health, Education, and Welfare, the lack of understanding of the problems of children has been spelled out.

Called "Analyzing Delinquent Behavior—a New Approach," the booklet argues that what is delinquent behavior for a white suburban child may be normal behavior for a youngster from the slums—whether urban or rural.

It was written by John M. Martin and Joseph P. Fitzpatric, professors of sociology at Fordham University, and by Dr. Robert E. Gould, a professor of psychiatry at New York University and senior psychiatrist in charge of adolescent services at Bellevue hospital psychiatric division.

Use of drugs admitted

"Delinquency in a given neighborhood is not simply the acting out of personality defects, but rather largely represents patterns of behavior that should realistically, because of cultural and other structural reasons, be expected to occur in that setting," they suggest.

They add that to really solve the problems of children it is probably necessary for professionals to "know the delinquent within the context of his own community. Otherwise you don't really know him at all."

This might help explain why so few psychiatrists are able to help delinquents in reform schools.

"The training of psychiatrists, psychologists, and social workers . . . is not geared to train practitioners to scrutinize human behavior from this perspective," the authors explain.

One of the most controversial areas at present is the heavy use of tranquilizing and antidepressant drugs on children in trouble. This is known as chemotherapy.

Drug danger pointed out

Two institutions, the Iowa Training School for Boys and the Juvenile Evaluation Center at Swannanoa, N.C., have used drugs most extensively.

In North Carolina I found many children getting hypodermic injections every two weeks and "booster" medication taken orally after meals. Officials explained that mental hospitals have been using these drugs "for over 15 years."

The drugs slow down overactive children, pep up those who are sluggish, says Harold W. Stephan, director of the clinical division at the center. He says it has cut the runaway rate, reduced fighting, and has helped children "become consistently happy."

"We have the most disturbed children in the juvenile correctional system," he says. "Many have serious emotional disorders."

While at the institution they participate in remedial reading, special education, vocational training, and other programs. Many youngsters, when they are released, are expected to continue taking the drugs indefinitely.

But some psychiatrists and physicians call the use of these drugs "dangerous," and others contend that it is an easy way out— that the youngsters on medication are turned into "zombies" who never come to grips with their problems.

Other experimentation

Experimenting on children in institutions is common—whether in the use of drugs, or with other forms of "treatment."

In California those from the behavioristic school of psychology are setting up an experiment at one school of 400 boys, while those who believe in insightive group therapy are working with another 400 at a companion school.

The behaviorists will try to change children with only material rewards — money, a pat on the back, whatever a child responds to. The theory seems to be that every child has his price, and if he is paid off he will do whatever the staff wants him to do.

The group therapists are interested in giving the boy insight into his "inner self" — believing that if a child gains this kind of knowledge he will be able to control himself.

Question raised

Both approaches are being used — without research attached — at scattered institutions around the country.

Richard Sowles, chief of psychological services at the Utah State Industrial School was quite candid. He said he took the low-paying job because he could experiment with children. He hoped this would help him gain a national name which could lead to a better position.

While many argue that this is the only way to learn how to deal with children in trouble, it raises questions about the use of children as guinea pigs.

Beyond the stopgaps . . .

Leaders in the correctional field generally agree that large institutions damage children, cause crime, and should be abandoned.

These institutions are to corrections what Edsels, Packards, and Hudsons are to the automotive industry—obvious failures. Yet state lawmakers keep building them.

With the public unready to bulldoze down traditional reform schools, some correctional administrators resort to stopgap solutions.

Making reform schools coeducational cuts homosexuality. In Washington boys are bused 18 miles from a forest camp for classes at the Maple Lane School for Girls. Girls also hold pizza parties and dances for boys in their cottages almost every weekend. There are no incidents.

The Weeks [reform] School in Vermont has long been coeducational. There, many youngsters go to public schools in town. Boys and girls who remain on campus are permitted to walk hand in hand without guards watching them.

In the Rhode Island Reform Schools for Boys and Girls an outstanding teaching staff has been assembled. Some children live in either the boys' or girls' school, yet hold jobs in the community. There are frequent field trips to sporting and cultural events. A variety of evening programs has been developed — a policeman teaches archery and weightlifting; the swimming pool is in constant use.

At the Connecticut School for Boys in Meriden (an otherwise grim institution) an experimental cottage has been in operation for more than three years—although those who run Cottage K are constantly battling traditionalists.

Scattered across the nation, one finds other examples of reform schools desperately trying to overcome the "big-institution syndrome."

But the answers, of course, lie elsewhere. These will be discussed in subsequent articles.

CHAPTER VII

'People here care about you'

**Here are some approaches to the juvenile correctional problem
which, while not panaceas, show positive results:
small institutions, individualized help, genuine "caring"—
and the recognition that delinquents can be helped.**

TWO ALUMINUM CANOES BOBBED BEneath soaring cliffs in the Buffalo River wilderness area in northern Arkansas. Redbud and dogwood blossoms sprinkled the humped hills like sequins on a green gown. Smoke from a campfire drifted through the warm April air. Small boys whooped happily as they rode hickory saplings to the ground.

A Boy Scout canoe trip?

No. Seven boys 10 to 12 years old. All in trouble or on the edge of trouble in Dallas. All failing in school.

In some cities they would be prime candidates for reform school. But not in Dallas. For they were spending 28 days away from home and school with two carefully selected adults — an outing sponsored by the Salesmanship Club of Dallas, and supported by both teachers and parents.

Two months earlier in the Rockies west of Denver 10 black street-gang members from Chicago's South Side, all in their late teens, fought their way through ice, snow, and stinging wind to the top of 13,000-foot Bison Peak.

The climb was part of a special 21-day course offered by the Colorado Outward Bound School. A private organization, Outward Bound normally provides adventurous summer trips for youngsters from middle-class and wealthy families.

Busy with chores

At the Yellowstone Boys Ranch, near Billings, Montana, boys fed cattle, swept out the academic school, worked in the dining room, slopped hogs, gathered eggs — all for pay. Most have savings accounts. If they insist, they can squander the money they earn and hopefully learn a lesson — just like most middle-class children.

At Boys Town, Neb., boys worked after school to earn money for clothing, soft drinks, after-shave lotion, and other extras.

Some worked on the farms. Others delivered papers, worked in the bowling alley, or the soda fountain.

Hundreds of miles to the east, in Syracuse, N.Y., children in trouble made their beds in their rooms in an old three-story apartment building owned by the New York State Division for Youth and then left for school or for work.

In neighboring Auburn hard-core delinquents living at a Division for Youth START (for short-term adolescent residential training) center painted a National Guard armory in a program that emphasizes community service.

On Staten Island, girls at a START center crossed the street to work in a hospital.

Near Ithica, N.Y., tough delinquents from the Bronx, Harlem, Brooklyn, and other rough areas stood knee-deep in snow happily wielding axes and saws for the conservation department.

Woods work for many

Teen-agers in trouble also were working in the woods in California, Washington, Ohio, Michigan, Connecticut, Illinois, and other states.

In New Jersey youngsters with long police records finished breakfast and then rode to a state hospital to empty bed pans and garbage cans and to do other chores.

At a former Nike missile base 30 miles west of Chicago, 80 delinquent boys between the ages of 9 and 14 attended a special school. There they were learning to read. They worked to catch up with students of the same age in public schools.

Scattered across the nation are other small state- or privately-run ranches, schools, and camps for boys and girls in trouble. Many provide promising alternatives to huge, grim institutions. Some are horrible.

In interviewing individuals who are most

When comfort is needed . . .

successful in helping children in trouble one finds agreement on three basic premises:

1. Almost all unacceptable behavior — whether stealing, lying, drinking, being promiscuous, the inability to perform in school, temper tantrums, withdrawal, and even hallucinating — is "learned." It is not innate and would not have developed under a different set of circumstances.

2. Thus, all children—given loving, individualized care that meets their needs—*can be helped.*

3. The best way to change delinquent behavior is to improve the environment that caused the behavior—the home and parents, the neighborhood, the school, the child's friends. Lacking the ability to do this, the only answer is to give the child strengths needed to cope with the destructive environment.

This is the promise of the small institution, which may succeed where so many traditional state-run institutions constantly fail.

When properly run by people with the right motives and goals, small institutions have several virtues:

● Sometimes they can reach children early, before they face the shock of being arrested, thrown in jail, or hauled into court. Once these things happen the job of rehabilitation becomes far more difficult — although the traumatic experience may jar some middle-class children into acceptable behavior.

● Instead of being "sent up," which clearly communicates to the child that he is "rotten," the child may play a role in choosing where he goes. This gives him incentive to succeed.

● Small institutions can be selective—accepting only children they feel confident they can help. This starts the child off right since he feels wanted, even privileged to be there. And the staff members expect the child to be helped.

● Small institutions may specialize, where large institutions too often must deal with all kinds of children from the normal to the retarded or deeply disturbed, from shrinking violets to animalistic brutes.

● With proper staffing, a small institution can give a child individualized attention. In large state institutions children become faceless numbers.

● Usually there is far less stigma attached to the small institutions.

● They save taxpayers money. Milton Luger, of the New York State Division for Youth, has estimated that group homes, for example, can cut the cost of institutional bed space in half; that group homes can be run a third cheaper than traditional reform schools.

No panaceas found

It must be emphasized that even the best small institution is no panacea.

Unfortunately the real answer—improving society with its destructive parents, schools, neighborhoods—is a long-drawn-out process. Thus stopgaps are needed. Small, specialized institutions appear to be the best available answer when the home and community fail.

This is the role filled by the Salesmanship Club in Dallas. Now made up of 450 business and professional men, it was founded in 1921. From the start the club has been interested in youngsters.

Since 1946, under the leadership of Campbell Loughmiller (now retired), emphasis has been on children in trouble—especially those with deep emotional disturbances.

Core of the program is a unique, rugged, year-round camp in northeastern Texas. Boys sleep out doors winter and summer in shelters they have built of canvas and saplings.

The camp is divided by age into four groups of 10 boys, with the youngest boys eight or nine years old. Each group is guided by two sensitive, rugged young college graduates, who may be trained in anything from chemistry to prelaw.

Two years a common stay

Youngsters stay in the program up to two years. During this period they will climb mountains, canoe, fish, hike, and learn to survive in the wilderness. Stress is placed on group therapy—a process of talking out individual or group problems as they develop.

This means stopping in the middle of a meal, or just before pushing canoes into the water — talking wherever and whenever problems arise until a solution is found.

The camp is backed up by social workers who deal with parents, and by an eight-boy halfway house in town for those who can't go home.

Two years ago, under the current executive director, Billy B. Trigg, Adventure Trails was added as an experiment to see if more boys could be helped with short-term programs. These boys hike, climb mountains, paddle canoes, or take 28-day trips down major rivers on rafts they have built.

Each group is limited to eight boys and headed by two young college graduates. Emphasis again is on teamwork, individual attention, and group therapy.

The current Salesmanship Club budget: $330,000. A third of that is raised by the annual exhibition game between the Dallas Cowboys and Green Bay Packers. The club nets another $50,000 from the Byron Nelson Golf Classic.

Income from the club's permanent investments brings in roughly $60,000. The United Fund once donated half the budget, but this year has been asked only for $35,000. Donations and dues bring in some money. And parents contribute what they can afford — from nothing up to $360 a month.

'Mix' of problems sought

Problems range from extreme withdrawal to aggressive delinquency. Mr. Trigg believes that for his program a "good mix," rather than trying to sort out boys by problems, is the answer.

Salesmanship boys have at least one thing in common: They are failing in school.

Yet, no formal educational program is involved—beyond planning menus, measuring quantities of food or floor space for a new shelter, reading maps, or writing reports and letters.

It is noteworthy that nearly every Salesmanship boy—regardless of length of stay—is able to return to school at the grade level normal for his age—almost as if he had never missed school. And he usually does far better than when he left school a year or two before.

Referrals come from many sources: the court, welfare department, mental health officials, schools.

The Salesmanship Club has been looking at the Outward Bound program as the club develops its short-term Adventure Trails. But Outward Bound, in turn, has learned from the Salesmanship Club, says Joseph J. Nold, director of the Colorado school.

A different approach

Outward Bound officials are reluctant to talk about their work with delinquents. Joshua Miner, III, president of Outward Bound, Inc., headquartered in Andover, Mass., explains that he "lives in deadly fear that we will be tagged as a school for delinquents." This would "frighten parents of normal, healthy kids" and "could kill us."

Outward Bound was *not* set up for children in trouble. It is a program for young men from middle-class and rich families who are looking for a chance to prove their manhood. The program lasts 26 days, and costs $400. Age limits are 16½ to 21. The course involves severe physical challenge—pushing a youth to his physical limits—coupled with teamwork and campfire bull sessions.

In Colorado the young men climb mountains; in Minnesota they go on canoeing expeditions in the Superior-Quetico Wilderness area; in Maine they sail 30-foot whaleboats. Each features a "solo"—three days' sur-

vival alone in the wilderness living off the land. This is "the best part of the program," says Mr. Nold.

"Something important happens to the boy. While alone he is encouraged to assess who he is, where he came from, where he is going."

The advantages such a program can offer youngsters in trouble are obvious. So, from time to time delinquents are quietly slipped into regular 12-member groups—almost always with startling success. Special delinquency programs are run separately during the winter months. Even then, without normal youngsters to help pull the less fortunate along, the results are impressive.

As in the Salesmanship program, staff is the key. Mr. Nold seeks out "sensitive, imaginative, tough, strong, masculine men." Even the most difficult boys quickly come to depend on these men—and relate in a positive way to them—when for the first time they stand at the foot of a mountain and begin to climb.

Court commitments tried

The Denver court has been committing delinquents to Outward Bound as an experiment — with good results. And the Maine Outward Bound school just completed its second winter developing an Overlander program at the Lyman School for Boys in Westboro, Mass.

New York has been pioneering in the field of small institutions and group homes through the State Division for Youth, headed by Mr. Luger.

The New York State Division for Youth, which operates independently of the correctional system, was formed in 1945 under another name. Until 1960 it distributed state funds to communities for street-gang workers, teen centers, and other facilities for young people.

In 1960 it began opening experimental homes and camps for 15-, 16- and 17-year-olds. It is still running most of them, though Mr. Luger says he is not interested in running a system that permanently parallels the correctional system. So far, a group home in Brooklyn and a START center in Amenia have already been turned over to the New York State Department of Social Services. Mr. Luger hopes that eventually various agencies will want to take over the others, so his team can move on to new areas.

Several small group homes are scattered around the state. They are for children who cannot live in their own homes.

START centers house 20 boys or girls for 4 to 14 months, some up to two years. Emphasis is on serving others.

The atmosphere is relaxed and open, al-

though most of the youngsters have been in serious trouble. Burglary, car theft, robbery, and assault are among the offenses.

Free time permitted

Many have committed more serious offenses than some youngsters found in the state reform schools. Yet the evening I visited the Auburn START center the boys were permitted to spend a half hour on their own in a shopping center while the superintendent, Calvin Weldon, and I talked in a restaurant. We had dropped three others off at an evening auto-mechanics course downtown.

Most Division for Youth programs include group therapy.

At the Austin MacCormick Youth Camp near Ithaca, boys work mornings for the Conservation Department and go to school in the afternoon. There is no lockup, no physical punishment.

"I useta go to the poolroom, cop a couple bags of smoke [marijuana], and go lookin' for trouble," says a 16-year-old Puerto Rican from Brooklyn. "I useta get sky high and really kick up a storm and didn't respect nobody. Now I don't do that no more, and I'm learnin' to respect others.

"They put a lota pressure on you here—treat you like a man. If they treated us like kids, then that's how we'd act."

Willis B. White, the superintendent, believes that if "the kids believe you really care what happens to them, then you can change them."

Sixty boys called ideal

Sixty boys live at the camp—about the ideal size, according to some experts.

More and more states are using forest camps as an alternative to a reform school or reformatory. It pays off.

The Highfields Residential Group Center in New Jersey is considered the model for small institutions using "angry" group therapy. When full, it accommodates 20 boys. These young men, usually with long police records, live in the old stone Charles A. Lindbergh house deep in the woods. During the days boys work at a state hospital.

Each evening before they go to bed they sit down and talk about themselves and others in the home.

A new boy will tell his "life story." That means he will discuss his criminal activity in detail. Then the other boys talk about why the youth is in trouble—explaining to him that while he may come from a deplorable home and poor neighborhood, he *is* responsible for his own actions.

Youngsters also discuss one another — the youth who mouths off; another who

does a poor job of making his bed or doesn't keep his room clean; a third who acts like a baby when under pressure; a fourth who has a hot temper.

Release based on progress

The boys must work on individual problems until they are mastered. Release is based on success of home visits and the decision of the other youths that a boy can handle himself without getting into further trouble.

The theory is that these meetings—the process is called guided group interaction—help a young man mature as he begins to understand his own behavior and that of others. And he learns better ways to deal with problems.

More and more institutions are using this type of group therapy. When the therapy is done effectively, officials say they are impressed with the results.

Florida's Division of Youth Services has opened two group homes, one only a few weeks ago. While still perfecting its program, the Walter Scott Criswell House in Tallahassee has had some remarkable successes.

Coming from extremely destructive environments, the boys there suddenly found people who cared deeply about them.

Don had been in reform schools three times. He recalled that he "was just a number. Here there are people to talk to, people who care about you. You can trust them. I learned that if I act different, then people act different toward me."

Don, now calm, steady, relaxed, is one of the most popular youths in the house.

Small camps, ranches, and private schools dot the map. Many are run by those who have been with church groups dealing with young people.

Ranch a 'longtime dream'

Franklin Robbie has run the Yellowstone Boys Ranch near Billings, Mont., for a dozen years. He was formerly a Youth for Christ worker and the ranch was a "longtime dream." It is licensed for 96 boys.

Older boys ride a school bus to town. For the younger boys, the ranch has its own school district. Classes are reduced to 12 students per teacher. The ranch involves about 320 acres, with 250 head of cattle in a feeder lot. A six-acre garden, hogs, chickens, and other livestock provide the institution with food. They often win ribbons at the state fair.

All youngsters are sent on court order. Arrivals range in age from 9 to 13. The majority are typical of those one finds in reform schools in an average state—some-

Safari to self-discovery

what delinquent or with severe problems at home. Boys stay from 2 to 2½ years.

The atmosphere is relaxed, and boys do not feel locked up. While they work hard, they also play hard—swimming in town, riding horses, camping, participating in league sports. Those who go to school in town are encouraged to participate fully in extracurricular activities.

'A real family wanted'

Dale, a rather disturbed child, is 13. His mother passed on before he was one, and his older sister when she was 18. Dale longs for a normal life. He lived with neighbors for a while, but his father refused to let them adopt him. He had been at the ranch 1½ years when I met him.

"I've always wanted a real family," he said wistfully. "I want so much to have a family and a home of my own. If I don't get it now I may never have a chance again."

These private institutions are usually the first choice of juvenile judges trying to decide what to do with children in trouble. But because of their small size, selectivity, and length of stay it is hard to find openings.

Many judges believe some of the 50 institutions run by the Sisters of the Good Shepherd are among the best for girls. While run by Roman Catholics, they accept girls of any faith, and Protestants are not forced to take regular courses in religion. The girls do study ethics and a "code of right living." They may be counseled by ministers of their own faith.

Villa St. Rose, in Portland, Ore., has the following standards: "Girls from 13 to 18 years of age, inclusive, regardless of race or creed, who have a minimum I. Q. of 85 and who have attained average school achievement. Girls whose physical or handicapping condition is such as to make the following of ordinary institution routines difficult or impossible—or who are pyromaniacs, suicidal, homosexual, or who require intensive, prolonged psychiatric care—are not accepted. We do not accept pregnant girls."

Careful selection attempted

Local officials add that because there are so many girls in need, the Portland home can be even more selective. Girls of high-school age with I.Q.s of 110 or above, and from a middle- or upper-middle-class family are preferred. All nuns are trained in social work. Counseling is available 24 hours a day.

Villa St. Rose has a capacity of 80 girls, but because of the great need for places for girls—even under the high standards—the home sometimes accepts 90 girls into its program.

Undoubtedly America's best-known private institution for children in trouble—one with a strong record of success—is Father Flanagan's Boys' Home in Boys Town, Neb. Interdenominational in its work, it was founded in 1917 by a Roman Catholic priest, Fr. Edward J. Flannagan, for "homeless and underprivileged boys, regardless of race, color, and creed." It admits boys between the ages of 10 and 16. Its literature states:

"Contrary to an opinion sometimes held, the Boys Town program is not designed to deal with the delinquent boy. Primarily, it is a preventive program, rather than a corrective one. A small percentage of all boys accepted at Boys Town have come from the courts, but not always because of delinquency. . . .

"When boys with a record of delinquency are accepted at Boys Town . . . it is because, in the opinion of the home, the delinquency stems from their homelessness or neglect, rather than from deep-seated emotional tendencies toward anti-social behavior. . . . The Boys Town program is designed for the normal boy, and facilities are not available for intensive medical or psychiatric care."

Demand far exceeds capacity

Each year the home receives some 3,500 applications. Less than 10 percent can be accepted. Capacity of the home is 900. To resolve the problem of size, Boys Town is divided into a grade-school section and high-school section. Each section is further divided into small units "to provide an opportunity to individualize the program."

Stress is on education — both academic and vocational. The vocational program is emphasized because so few of each year's graduates are able to go on to college or enter business.

Before a boy graduates from high school, job placement is arranged for him.

Not all private institutions measure up to the high standards of Boys Town. It is extremely difficult to discover which do and which do not. There is little or no inspection or evaluation going on.

While many private institutions screen out society's worst problem children — those severely disturbed, those classified as mentally retarded, and the tough delinquents— a few specialize in these children, and may charge $8,000 to $12,000 per year per child. Obviously this is out of reach of most families—even when there are openings available.

In addition to the new, small state camps and schools and private institutions working with children in trouble, there are county facilities scattered across the nation. These are sometimes far superior to state institutions, though not always.

One of the most interesting is the Los Palmas School for Girls, run by Los Angeles County.

The school is limited to 100 girls—10 to a cottage. Each cottage has a woman college graduate staff member present when the girls are awake; and even the night staff must have two years' college experience.

In addition to this, the school has 15 staff members with master of social work degrees, plus five consulting psychiatrists and two consulting psychologists.

Dorothy Kirby, superintendent of the school, says 75 percent of the girls have tried drugs and 20 to 30 percent of these have tried to commit suicide. They are products of broken and destructive homes.

"Over 15 percent of the girls in this institution today have had an incestual relationship," she adds. "Out of every 100 we get, 15 to 20 have been involved, usually with their fathers. We get children who have been victimized for years."

To solve these problems the school has adopted family group therapy. Groups consist not only of one family, but also eight or nine families at once — partly so they don't feel so guilty in their failure, seeing others have failed, and partly because they can help each other.

But not all parents can stand the confrontation, nor do all girls have parents.

In addition to high-caliber staff, the school has a strong compulsory academic program, a swimming pool, bicycles, a canteen for refreshments and other items the girls want, arts and crafts, and coeducational activities.

Each girl has a private room and can have a radio, record player, personal bulletin board, and other normal teen-age items. Male staff members have also been added to the program and this has been found helpful.

Los Angeles also has 11 camps for boys in the foothills of the mountains, all tied to the Probation Department. The two I visited had a capacity of 94 boys—one for boys 16 to 18, another for smaller boys. But these camps lack staff.

Views differ on group therapy

Renso Y. Enkoji, director of Camp Afflerbaugh — for older boys — is deeply opposed to group therapy, and it is not used at his school.

Caring' can turn delinquents around

"I think it is very poor. It tears kids apart. Egos are ill-formed. I'm opposed to all this verbalization, and suspect that slick answers are turning children into sociopaths.

"The adolescent kid loves action. Let him enjoy it. Let him feel it."

The camp takes boys with higher I.Q.s than those in most other camps. Emphasis is on education, plus four hours' work in parks and golf courses. The program resembles that of military schools, where more wealthy parents send their children in trouble. Mr. Enkoji is willing to take delinquents but prefers to avoid accepting emotionally disturbed children.

For children who are immature, impulsive, hyperactive, perhaps the greatest value of the mountain camp is the quiet. The rush and noise of the city is behind them. A very complex world full of problems has become simplified.

But in many states, county camps and schools, like large institutions, are too often ignored by the public. Seldom are there standards. Too many are underfunded.

Yet many experts believe that they hold far more promise than huge reform schools —if they are properly staffed and funded.

The consensus is that construction of huge state facilities must be stopped. Those that exist should take in only children from neighboring counties to make it easier to work with the families involved. Then these institutions should be broken down into smaller units that can meet the child's individual need—much as a large university is divided into specialized schools.

This is being done in scattered places. The brightest spot at the Connecticut School for Boys in Meriden is Cottage K, an experimental unit that has taken in some of the toughest youths in the institution.

Weekend outings frequent

It was developed by Dr. Earl S. Patterson, a psychiatrist, nearly four years ago. The day I visited the institution, there were 18 boys there — plus carefully selected staff members. The goal is not to make children adjust to an institution, but rather to take the child into the community and teach him how to live there without getting into more trouble.

Dr. Patterson believes in dealing with reality. But the child's reality of slum living or an alcoholic or otherwise destructive parent is different from what most people experience. So Dr. Patterson tries to improve the child's concept of reality.

This is done, in part, through taking the boys on outings — getting them off the grounds, especially on weekends when there is so little to do. The boys go horseback riding, to movies, to sporting and cultural events. Four youngsters are attending school in town, others are working off the grounds.

They build boats, learn to drive, take Red Cross life-saving classes — anything constructive that will help them in the community. Boys are given much of the responsibility for decisionmaking, and in fact have even curtailed swearing on their own.

"We are trying to build a nondelinquent culture here," Dr. Patterson says. "This is difficult within the larger culture of the institution, which fosters delinquency. A surprising number of boys are hit by staff members—more even than we had realized" [before this newspaper's investigation of conditions].

Echo Glen, near Seattle, has an impressive staff—including many energetic young men and women. Fourteen workers have master's degrees in social work. There are 215 staff members for 208 youngsters. Staff members work in teams when children are not asleep or in school. There is one worker on duty at all times for every eight children. A full-time physician and full-time dentist are on the staff.

The setting is probably the most beautiful in America—a campus in the mountains 30 miles east of Seattle. A man-made lake is stocked with trout. Each 16-child, two-wing cottage has a large central fireplace. Children are constantly busy with constructive activities. The school has an excellent library, indoor swimming pool, chapel, vocational programs.

Some prefer the camp

Many who are committed prefer the camp to their unpleasant homes. I met one girl at another reform school in the state who said she had broken the law after being released from Echo Glen in hopes of being sent back there.

Emphasis at Echo Glen is on working with families, so that the home can be less damaging to the child.

This is a key to success at all institutions —the quality of the parole (or after-care) program. But in almost all states parole is severely neglected. Children don't get the assistance they need—jobs, help in school, help at home, support for their parents.

Yet there are bright spots. Parole for juveniles in Montana is unusually good. But more workers are needed.

In South Carolina, where reform schools are poor, there is a surprisingly good after-care program—though it, too, is understaffed. Citizens in Charleston, S.C., have established the first halfway house in that state. More are needed across the nation.

Sherwood Norman, director of youth correction services of the National Council on Crime and Delinquency, suggests that institutions should have no more than 150 youngsters enrolled, although "for purposes of treatment none should be larger than 50."

William H. Sheridan, of the Children's Bureau in Washington, part of the Department of Health, Education, and Welfare, sums it up this way:

"A state agency into whose care delinquent children are committed needs to work not only for the diversification of its resources for treatment and care but also for the development and improvement of local community services."

This will take place only with citizen concern.

"Sawing the bars off the windows"

Harry Vorrath, a former marine, policeman, law student, seminarian, and in recent years social worker with a master's degree, strongly believes large correctional institutions should be shut down. But he also believes there **are** answers within their framework as long as such institutions exist.

Mr. Vorrath was given the opportunity to prove that his ideas worked with small groups in Kentucky, Washington, D.C., and in scattered spots across the country. The projects were successful. He was able to turn small groups of tough delinquents around. But Mr. Vorrath wanted to try his program at a large institution.

He got his chance last fall after things fell apart at a better-than-average reform school in Red Wing, Minn. Youngsters rioted and ran. Mr. Vorrath was called in.

Using a technique that might be described as building a culture of caring, Mr. Vorrath divides the boys into groups of 10 each. Every member of each group is responsible for all the boys in his group. Thus positive peer pressure helps delinquents learn to care for themselves and others.

Fortunately, Mr. Vorrath had the strong support of Superintendent Milton S. Olson and his staff. They turned the institution around in seven months. Runs have nearly stopped, along with other problems. It was done without staff members beating youngsters. More important, depressed, hating boys have been turned into young men who care.

"I'm one of the old-time guys here," says white-haired Mike Reier.

"I used to think the only way to handle these boys was to crack heads, to use force to make them behave. And to prove it, I've got a bad leg that came from a tussle with two boys.

"I've never seen anything like this. I used to watch the boys every minute. Now they go out and cut the grass without supervision. We've been letting the boys saw the bars off the windows."

Edward Bruggenman, also a longtime employee, puts it this way: "For the first time we've really got something to work with and to work for."

Mr. Vorrath believes that this "something" is teaching tough, troubled boys to care deeply enough for each other so that they will help each other to stop "hurting themselves and others."

His program is built on love—"not the sweet, sugar-coated kind," he adds. "I'm talking about the unselfish love that makes a marine crawl on his belly into enemy fire to save a wounded buddy."

Mr. Vorrath began to develop his program while working with tough delinquents at Highfields in New Jersey, where group therapy was pioneered.

There can be little doubt that the program works. At Red Wing, a few days ago, a reporter talked to boys sprawled on the lawn playing chess on a warm Sunday afternoon. Others batted a baseball around—all without supervision. The boys learn to help each other stay out of trouble.

Two-, three-, and four-time losers agree that before Mr. Vorrath arrived they could "con" the staff into letting them go home by pretending to conform to institutional requirements. No attitudinal improvement took place.

All this is changing. Under Mr. Vorrath's program, youngsters can't return to the community until they learn to care.

"We decide when it's time for a guy to go home," said one 15-year-old, who has been in institutions for a third of his life. "You can't con a con."

There are still important questions to be answered. Will Mr. Vorrath's culture of caring—what one finds in a strong, happy family—last after Mr. Vorrath has moved on to other institutions? Can he teach others to build this culture? And can youngsters so absorb this philosophy of caring deeply for others that they can survive on their own in the harsh, dog-eat-dog world they came from?

Minnesota has given Mr. Vorrath a chance to prove that all this can happen.

CHAPTER VIII

Who are the real delinquents?

Delinquents are made, not born. Who makes them?
Too often, the parents — through neglect, cruelty, selfishness,
or ignorance. Yet it is the child, not the parent, who
pays the penality. Simplistic solutions, however, solve nothing.
Jailing delinquent parents makes little more sense than
jailing their children. The solution lies in finding
ways to improve the parents.

WE OUGHT TO LOCK UP THE PAR-
ents instead of the kids."

As one probes the appalling world of children in trouble, he hears this statement
repeated again and again.

Reform-school superintendents say it.
Teachers and social workers say it. So do
policemen, psychologists, psychiatrists,
judges, probation officers, and prison chap-
lains.

This newspaper's study indicates that
most of those who work with children in
trouble are convinced that these youngsters
— whether in reform schools, mental hospitals, or other institutions — are products
of their environment. Their unacceptable
behavior is "learned."

In this learning process, the parents are
the first teachers. Peer groups, a bad neighborhood, even schoolteachers and policemen, may later contribute to the process.
But the parents usually set the mold, either
through action or inaction.

Based on a year-long study, including hundreds of interviews with both children and
experts, this newspaper has found:

1. Most children in trouble have an extremely poor self-image. Too often their
parents are "losers," unable to make a
marriage go, unsuccessful in business, or
are alcoholics, emotionally unstable, or have
other problems.

Communication difficult

2. Troubled youngsters find it nearly impossible to communicate their feelings in a
normal way to adults. Running away, striking out violently, giving up in school, and
other unacceptable forms of behavior may
simply be ways of saying, "Care about me,"
or "I can't cope."

Somewhere, somehow, somebody failed

3. Instead of dealing with children in
trouble appropriately, parents cry, nag,
bluster, call the child a "dummy" or worse,
and generally undermine the child's self-
concept.

4. Contrary to public opinion, most children in trouble have been spanked or beaten
over and over again with only negative results.

5. Many children become delinquent for
the first time after a shattering crisis in
home involving the parents. This may be a
divorce, separation, or death.

6. It is not the single-parent home that
causes delinquency or emotional unbalance
and other problems. Tens of thousands of
widows and divorced women have successfully raised youngsters without a man in the
home. Rather it is the inability or unwilling-
ness of a parent (and often the children) to
adjust to her new status.

7. Some divorced parents constantly be-
rate their ex-partners. When a child mis-
behaves he or she is told, "You are just like
your no-good father [or mother]." Mothers
may whine or cry a great deal.

Some parents baby the children — preventing them from emotionally growing up.
Others — trying to prove that they are still
"desirable" to the other sex — become promiscuous, and the children learn of this.

Still others, trying to "make up" for the
loss, may smother a child in gifts and
favors, or refuse to discipline the child in a
constructive way. Others overdiscipline or
overprotect the child, or become cold and
rejecting.

Judges' actions a factor

8. The conditions that drove the spouse
away and resulted in divorce — bad habits,

extreme self-centeredness, inability to cope, or gross ignorance — may be the very thing that also drives the child to delinquency. Thus judges who automatically award the children to a mother — without any comprehension of the real reasons for the divorce, may contribute to the crime rate.

9. The child who is not properly prepared for the remarriage of a parent may rebel by breaking the law. Stepparents may be destructive if they do not understand or care about the stepchildren. Or the child may feel he is competing with the stepparent for his natural parent's "love." This can result in what social workers call "acting out." Some children "act out" by running. Others "escape" by sniffing glue, taking drugs, or indulging in other forms of defiant behavior.

10. Thousands of children in trouble come from what appear to be "normal" homes. But probe beneath the surface, and one may find alcoholism, emotional unbalance, a namby-pamby or violent father, or other problems. Some children face inconsistent controls—with one parent extremely permissive, the other very rigid. Others cannot live up to models set by an older brother or sister; are under constant pressure to do better in school; or are constantly being compared with "good" children in the neighborhood.

Neighborhood roots common

11. When an older brother or sister gets in trouble, often the younger children will also become delinquent. This happens for a variety of reasons: the conditions that produced the first delinquent probably have not changed; younger children often admire an older child and want to "be like him." Teachers, neighbors, and police (even parents) may expect the younger children to turn out bad. Thus they treat these nondelinquent youngsters like a delinquent—with the expected results.

12. Neighborhoods which parents feel forced into, because of poverty or prejudice, produce children in trouble. If youngsters see prostitution, alcoholism, gambling, and crime wherever they turn, they grow up without knowing there is something better. Delinquent behavior becomes only what seems natural.

13. Some middle-class parents strive so hard for financial or social success that they neglect their children or give them "things" instead of what they really need—proper love and guidance.

14. Frequent corporate transfers may also lead to delinquency if certain other factors are present. The child who lacks parental support and does not make friends easily sometimes joins the first group that accepts him. This group may be involved in deviant behavior—drinking, drug use, promiscuity, skipping school, or shoplifting, and so on.

15. Parents addicted to TV may contribute to delinquency by confining family activities to television watching. This can limit family communication to "be quiet" or "wait until the program is over if you want to ask me something." Eventually the child goes elsewhere for answers, or forces parents to pay attention by misbehaving.

Peer groups important

16. The opinions of other young people are extremely important to most teen-agers. Without a strong parent-child relationship, the "group" or the "gang" will almost always win out. Some youngsters who have lost battles with parents about hair styles, jewelry, or clothing keep outfits unacceptable to parents at a friend's house or in a school locker. Other things may be hidden from parents. This conflict with parents and double life may result in parents' losing control and serious problems.

17. A high percentage—estimates vary from 10 percent up to a third or more—of girls in trouble have had incestual relationships with their fathers or stepfathers.

18. Many other girls in trouble are so hungry for attention or affection that they become sexually involved with "the first fellow who comes along and pretends to care," the experts add.

19. Parents who constantly excuse misbehavior—and through manipulation, bluster, bribe, or threat put down neighbors, school officials, policemen, or judges—may eventually see their children behind bars.

20. Parental immaturity — usually expressed in extreme selfishness, lack of consistency, cruel teasing, or inappropriate discipline—may cause problem children.

21. Refusing to let teen-agers grow up, the overprotective parent can also cause problems. For when the rigid family bond is broken, some children run wild.

22. Conversely, inadequate supervision frequently leads to delinquency, too. Parents encourage sexual promiscuity, use of narcotics or alcohol, and other problems by leaving children home alone. Interviews with youngsters in training schools across the country indicate that many got into trouble in their own or other children's homes — often when the mother works.

Many mistakes shaken off

Many of the foregoing do not of themselves cause delinquency. Obviously there is no such thing as a perfect parent. Lapses in discipline, affection, interest occur in the best of homes. Fortunately, children are highly resilient and usually shake off minor parental mistakes.

It is only the extreme parental abuses—constant rejection, alcoholism, incest, brutal beatings — that by themselves cause delinquency and emotional instability. And this reporter has found that even children who have been treated brutally or who have parents with severe problems usually talk of their strong love for their mothers and fathers. A child's yearning for affection enables him to forgive much. Sometimes this yearning may not give way to disillusionment and bitterness until the late teens.

It is easy to generalize about "causes," or to substitute one simplistic solution for another ("lock parents up instead of the children"). But when one begins to look at individual cases and apply existing knowledge or techniques, it becomes clear why the problems of children in trouble so often go unsolved.

Divorce soon followed

Take Jimmy, a bright-eyed, red-headed 10-year-old from the Los Angeles area. His mother, escaping from an unpleasant home, was married at the age of 17 in November, 1956. She lived with her husband a month before she discovered he was already married. Jimmy was born 8½ months later.

Jimmy's mother remarried in June, 1958, when he was 1½ years old. Her new husband drank heavily and beat Jimmy with his open hand, his fist, and a belt. In a fit of rage in 1963 he threw a bowling ball at the boy.

Jimmy's mother, who by now had two more sons, divorced this second husband a few months later. He disappeared. He made no support payments, a common occurrence. Soon she went to the Welfare Department for help.

She was a proud woman. Having read constant criticism of "lazy welfare mothers" in the newspapers, she decided to go to work. Having married early, she had no special skill. She found a night job as a waitress and with tips made slightly more than what she had received while on welfare.

For a few weeks she paid a neighbor roughly half her wages to watch the children until she got home from work at 11:30 at night. But soon her neighbor grew weary of the work. Besides, Jimmy's mother found she couldn't pay both the baby sitter and the landlord.

Yet she liked the job. She was making new friends and she was out of the apartment, where she had had too much time to think about her troubles. More important, she was meeting men again. Perhaps the boys soon might have another father.

Instead of quitting, she fixed supper each night before she went to work and left Jimmy in charge of his two half-brothers. The children often were found wandering alone around the neighborhood well after dark.

Welfare stepped in

In late 1965 the Welfare Department stepped in and took her to court. The judge was appalled that not only was she leaving the children alone but that she brought male strangers home from work. He called her a "common pick-up."

She could not afford a lawyer, nor could she, with her lower-class background and abbreviated education, find the words to make the judge understand her plight.

The three boys were found neglected, taken from her, and placed in foster homes.

Jimmy's foster parents were decent enough—they just didn't know how to handle a boy who had a need for love and care even while asserting the independence he had grown accustomed to while his mother worked nights.

Besides, he missed his mother desperately; worried about her constantly. The forced separation made him angry, hostile.

Nor did his foster parents know what to do when he began, in the spring of 1966, to steal bicycles. He was arrested for taking six. Soon he was shifted to another foster home.

He "hated" the new foster parents, who lived differently from both his real mother and the other foster parents. Jimmy ran away. He found a car with the keys in it. Police, noticing a small boy hardly able to poke his head up high enough to see through the windshield, arrested him. He was put in a detention home.

The judge lectured him, but Jimmy didn't listen. He felt adults could not be trusted. Besides, it was a judge who had taken him from his mother in the first place.

In September of 1966, Jimmy was back in court for stealing candy, cigarettes, and a toy plane. The judge was disgusted, the foster parents had "had it," so Jimmy was moved again.

He liked his new foster parents better: He stayed six months, until March of 1967, before running away after an argument over a dollar missing from the foster mother's purse. He was picked up, returned to his foster parents.

On May 1, after having trouble with a teacher, he ran again. It was raining and cool, and all he had worn to school was a short-sleeved shirt. So he stopped off at a shopping center and stole a jacket. He was caught. The manager, tired of so much shoplifting, demanded action. The court was tired of dealing with Jimmy and shipped him off to reform school.

When he "served his time" he was released to another foster home. In a few weeks he stole a car. He had learned to "hot wire" an ignition while locked up.

Who should go to court?

Jimmy's case, while more complicated than some, is fairly typical of that of many children in trouble.

Whom should society blame? Who should go to court?

Jimmy's mother for marrying too young and for the wrong reasons—marrying an already married man she hardly knew? The law doesn't cover that.

And what of Jimmy's father? Tracking him down and putting him in prison would "teach him a lesson." But how would it help the boy? It would cost the state more than supporting Jimmy on welfare.

The same is true of Jimmy's stepfather. Since he did not adopt Jimmy, his responsibility for Jimmy's support can be challenged.

He *is* responsible for the other two children. The court can put him in prison, too— but it can't make him work if he prefers to serve time.

If he has remarried and is making a go of it, then locking him up would only add another family to the welfare rolls and perhaps increase the number of delinquent children.

Perhaps, because of the three children, the second marriage should have been blocked. Had the second husband been applying for the role of foster parent or had he been trying to get a child from an adoption agency he would have been carefully screened. Why are stepfathers so different?

But will society, with its high divorce rate, let legislators pass such a law? On what grounds could such a marriage be blocked? The stepfather beat the children. But society condones corporal punishment by parents. Drunkenness in one's home also remains commonplace — even socially acceptable in middle-class society.

One can also ask about the responsibility of Jimmy's grandparents on both his mother's and father's side. One set apparently pushed their daughter into a hasty marriage. The other raised a son who could not tell right from wrong.

Present laws hold few answers that will help Jimmy. Nor are there laws to protect the child from an indulgent parent who may give him everything he asks for, yet doesn't know how to give love. How can the law teach a parent how to love?

Mary is 16, with short, blond hair. She ran away from her home in Albany four times. The last time she ran with a 21-year-old man and lived with him three months "right in Albany."

"I like it better here [at the reform school in Hudson, N.Y.] than at home," she says. "They spoiled me a lot, I guess. Up here I feel bad because they still send me things — things I don't deserve. But I don't think they love me.

'Younger sister favored'

"Oh, they'd say I did good in school, but they'd never say what I did good. I don't get along with my dad. And it seemed like they favored my younger sister more than me.

"They don't try to understand you. They never just sit down and talk to you about things like personal problems. I don't even know how to talk to them.

"I guess the thing that bothered me most was they didn't hug me. They keep sending me things here, but if they'd come for a visit and just hug me once, maybe things would be different."

Most states have laws that permit parents to take difficult children to court and send them to reform school. This is shocking, since there is strong evidence that the problems of children are usually caused by the parents.

In New York, one often finds "persons in need of supervision." Other states may list such children as incorrigible. Massachusetts has a "stubborn-child law" which funnels many youngsters into reform school.

Patrick A. Creeden, superintendent of John Augustas Hall, in West Boylston, Mass., where boys 7 to 12 are housed, says: "Most of our youngsters are more neglected than delinquent. The courts have adjudicated them delinquent on a stubborn-child complaint. There are no controls in the home, and the kids are running wild.

"Many youngsters are here for running away from a bad environment. They may have an alcoholic father or a promiscuous mother. The youngster may rebel at his mother bringing all these guys home. The judge commits them here to get them out of that environment."

Take Emily, a 15-year-old I met in the reform school for girls in New Mexico. She is the oldest of four children and rather plain. Her parents were divorced when she was 12 after her father "fell in love" with a woman he met in a bar. Her mother became involved with another man.

Emily began having trouble in school and was caught drinking with a gang of older youngsters. The court placed her in a series of foster homes. Her behavior got worse.

When her mother remarried Emily was returned home—only to be picked up for drinking again. She also refused to come home on time, and she said she didn't like her stepfather.

Her mother told the court that she simply could not control the girl. And so the youngster was sent off to reform school as an incorrigible child.

Nothing, of course, happened to the parents.

Some only 3 months old

Perhaps most difficult to understand is the parent who physically injures his children.

Dr. Richard Galdston, a Harvard Medical School professor of psychiatry, gathered data on battered children and their families for five years. He wrote in the American Journal of Psychiatry in October, 1966:

"Physical abuse should be distinguished from parental neglect. Many abused children are well-fed and cared for. It is striking to see a young child, covered with welts and bruises, all decked out in a fresh pinafore."

The abused children he studied ranged in age from 3 months to 3½ years. An X-ray would sometimes show "old, healed fractures of the ribs, skull, head, or of the humerus [shoulder]."

Dr. Galdston found most parents were young with limited income and education.

"Many of the fathers were unemployed or worked part-time, often alternating with their wives, who also worked. The wife cared for the child part of the time and worked the rest, relegating the care of the child to the husband or baby sitter. In appearance and demeanor many of the women were quite masculine and their husbands correspondingly passive and retiring."

Dr. Galdston said that the parents somehow thought of infants having the ability to reason and act as adults, and that most of the parents had bitter childhood experiences.

Some youngsters never have a chance.

Terrence is a 10-year-old Negro who was born in a Massachusetts mental hospital and was given to an elderly woman who was on welfare. He was committed on May 23, 1968, from Boston as a "stubborn child" when the woman, an alcoholic, died.

Terrence's mother had been the same when she was abandoned at age 3. By age 10 Terrence's mother was "stealing, setting fires, and having serious problems at school." She was placed in a series of institutions and private homes, was sent to the reform school while carrying Terrence, and was transferred to a mental hospital. She also served time in the women's reformatory and was jailed in Boston as a prostitute and for drunkenness.

One incident after another

Terrence once was placed with a great aunt who "loves the boy" but is too crippled to care for him. He lived there with his mother briefly, when she was not locked up, and was successfully involved in a prekindergarten program. Then his mother left "and he started acting up, failing in school." He "couldn't adapt to the group, had temper tantrums."

Terrence "roamed the streets of Boston, begging and stealing," picking through garbage cans to find something to eat.

When he was eight, two men picked him up in a car, apparently for immoral purposes. The record shows that they pushed him out of the car "on a main highway" where he was "hit by an oncoming car and then picked up by police and taken to a hospital."

The court tried to place him in six private institutions in New England. All turned Terrence down, stating they "could not cope with his behavior."

One can, by arousing the apathetic public, improve horrible jails, detention homes, reform schools, prisons, and institutions for the homeless, the mentally retarded, and the emotionally ill.

One can, by informing the public of the need, find compassionate people willing to open their homes to children in trouble.

This has been made clear by the flood of mail in response to this series.

But what can be done for the family?

If, as the evidence indicates, children in trouble come from parents in trouble, the solution would appear to be: resolve the parents' troubles. This is no easy task in a society where individual rights are sacred and the sanctity of the home must be preserved.

Yet the task, however challenging, is not hopeless when people care deeply. What is needed is a national effort—beginning at the neighborhood level—to help families help themselves.

When peers take over from parents

Almost as important as the family to a child's development is the peer group (other youngsters) he associates with. But the family a child comes from often determines the kind of peer group he chooses—or is forced to "choose." This, in turn, can determine whether he ends up "in trouble."

During a year's research for this series of articles, the author has drawn several conclusions about the role of the peer group:

• It is as hard to generalize accurately about young people—even those in trouble —as it is to generalize about adults. Each child's experience is unique. Yet all children have certain common needs that must be met by their parents and the larger world around them. These include love, understanding, and status. As one moves from childhood into adolescence, he also needs the opportunities to grow up.

• Social scientists see some conflict between adults and teen-agers as "normal." Adolescents must find some way to break parental ties and to develop their individualism.

• It is also normal for more idealistic youngsters to become angry at the hypocrisy, stupidity, and dishonesty they find in adult society—especially when adults seem more tolerant of society's flaws than of the young people who want to correct those flaws.

• While adults rail at youngsters for conforming to a peer group, this behavior again is normal. Adults also conform to peer pressures. Businessmen wear white shirts and ties when other clothing might be more comfortable. Couples learn to play bridge, so they can be part of a group. Others may feel obligated to attend a cocktail party, when they would prefer to spend a quiet evening at home.

Many confused, middle-class Americans put all teen-agers in the same "bag." Seeing a boy with long hair, they may conjure up visions of barricaded campus buildings; bearded motorcyclists terrorizing towns; glassy-eyed hippies sprawling semiconscious in cold-water flats; or angry blacks robbing, beating, or rioting.

Yet this long-haired youth may be an honor student whose only contact with "grass" is the lawn he obediently cuts for his parents.

• Just as parents shape—for good or ill— the behavior of the small child, so the peer group wields tremendous influence over the teen-ager. Again this part of growing up— testing ideas, learning to make decisions, becoming independent of parents, feeling accepted—is normal. These peer groups may be either positive or negative in their influence.

• Almost all delinquent youngsters, when they got in trouble for the first time, were with other youngsters. Many—especially those in the middle class—stole for the first time, used drugs, skipped school, or became involved in sex either on a dare or at a club or gang initiation. These newly delinquent youths then involved more youngsters in ever-widening circles of delinquency. Thus one child in trouble can, if the conditions are right, eventually contaminate a number of children in a wide area.

• Conversely, a delinquent may be reformed when a youngster moves into a better neighborhood—if the child's family is fairly stable and the children in that neighborhood accept the child into their group.

• When he has a choice, the group a teen-ager selects generally mirrors the youth's view of himself—a self-concept acquired when he was younger. A youth with a good opinion of himself will pick a "good" peer group—if such a group is available. When he says, "I don't like" certain youngsters, he really means "I don't feel comfortable with them." What they do or say may conflict with what he has been taught by his parents.

• Problems arise in urban slums and some rural areas when the only group available is delinquent. Beyond this, snobbish parents usually produce snobbish children— and some good youngsters may be excluded from "good" peer groups because of this.

Children also may exclude themselves for a variety of reasons. A child accepted by a group may drop out because he lacks money or clothing to keep up with his peers. He may find this lack embarrassing. When much is made of big homes and cars a child from a poor or filthy home may exclude himself from a peer group—again from embarrassment.

• Children with inadequate homes may leave to adopt a deviant peer group—that is, a street or motorcycle gang or a group of hippies—as a "family." This is often the case with runaway girls.

Interviewing youngsters who have done this, one finds the youth also may be torn between two clearly opposing value systems. A youngster sees the "middle-class bag" of two cars and a garage and concern over crabgrass as futile, while the excitement of the free and easy life is alluring.

It must be pointed out that the typical child in trouble seldom follows fads like long hair and weird dress. This behavior is more often found in restless middle-class youngsters who have too much spending money. Most children in trouble are fighting for survival. With some exceptions, one finds that jails, reform schools, mental hospitals, and prisons are generally reserved for the children of the poor.

He may simply be saying "care about me"

CHAPTER IX

America's priorities

Asked why delinquency thrives in the United States,
juvenile experts point to a headlong society bent on dollars
and self-gratification. A nation that can find billions for
autos, liquor, tobacco, war, and pets but skimps on its
children, needs to rethink its priorities.

JUVENILE DELINQUENCY WILL
thrive in the United States as long as basic
flaws in American society exist. This is the
consensus of professionals dealing with children
in trouble interviewed for this series.

These experts — from nearly every state,
and representing a wide variety of disciplines—see
many Americans as unthinking,
uncaring, and superselfish — a people who
desperately pursue dollars and self-gratification.

All generalizations are flawed. Yet this
newspaper's study shows that not only do
many citizens turn their backs on children
in trouble, but they also provide a climate
that makes crime and vice flourish.

Take Mary, a handsome 16-year-old white
girl from Seattle. Both her mother and
her father (a sometimes construction
worker) are alcoholics.

I met Mary in the Maple Lane School for
Girls. It was her second commitment.

Maturing early, Mary became a professional
prostitute at the age of 13. Her clients
were largely business and professional men,
although she also saw some prosperous blue-collar
workers.

She said she intends to return to prostitution
when she finishes "serving my time,"
for she sees it as her pass key to what her
clients' daughters have: fine clothing, a decent
place to live, good food, an expensive
car.

Trouble ran in the family

What turned Mary to prostitution? Perhaps
no one really knows. But one can
chronicle the events that led up to it.

From the start her parents lived in "bad
places"—shacks with roofs that leaked and
in noisy housing projects. Most of the children
she knew were from families in
trouble.

Juveniles have no lobby

Mary was deprived of all of the things a
little girl needs—love, attention, proper discipline,
decent clothing, good food.

Beaten with a belt, left to roam the
streets, it was obvious to her teachers that
this dirty, ragged child was in serious
trouble. But nothing was done about it.
When she disrupted a class she was sent
to the principal's office.

One of her older sisters was arrested
when she tried to walk out of a department
store with a stolen suit on. Another older
sister ran away from home and was never
seen again. An older brother was sent to reform
school.

Clearly a family in trouble. Yet no community
organization stepped in to help. No
church provided assistance. No governmental
agency intervened—except to make
arrests.

Starved for toys, candy, clothing, and the
other things most little girls get from their
parents, Mary began stealing from stores
when she was 10.

But her first contact with the police came
when at 12 she started a fire in a vacant lot.
To the police it was just another incident—
one "cleared by apprehension."

After that Mary had a number of minor
brushes with the police. She was picked up
wandering the streets late at night; was
caught shoplifting; frequently skipped
school. Her father was jailed in a break-in.
Her drunken mother constantly beat her.

Locked up in detention home

Eventually, at the age of 13, she was
locked up in the detention home in Seattle.
There she learned about prostitution from
one of the older girls—a homosexual. The
girl told Mary of big money she could make.
She gave Mary the address of a man who
would help her get started.

As soon as Mary was released she went to the address, and it wasn't long before she was earning "big money," buying expensive clothing. She also began using drugs.

Mary detests the men she serves. It is the money—and the things the money will buy—that keeps her at it.

Nor is Mary's story unusual. Not only are there girls at Maple Lane with similar backgrounds, but I also found hundreds like her in institutions scattered across the nation.

Are the children in trouble to blame?

The experts point out the obvious: Adults engage vulnerable children in prostitution. Adults produce and sell the drugs that turn children into addicts. Adults run the saloons and brew and sell the beverages that turn parents into alcoholics. They make drinking glamorous through advertising. They write and sell the magazines, books, movies, and television shows that provide young people a model for behavior—material which sometimes suggests that crime, sadism, promiscuity, war, and other forms of killing are "normal."

Middle-class adults also decide what acts are delinquent. When drug taking was limited to other people's children, use of marijuana was considered a crime deserving a long prison term. Now that the drug has moved into "good" neighborhoods, there is a growing cry to legalize its use.

But this is only part of the story.

Earnings compared

To understand why American society produces so many delinquents one has only to look to the nation's heroes.

Few, if any, schoolteachers, policemen, probation officers, scout leaders, YMCA instructors, ministers, or social workers are singled out for national honors. Nor are they paid adequately for the services they provide.

Historically, the most important medals have gone to explorers and to those who have been skilled at war.

Financial rewards have followed a different pattern. Before democracy, wealth belonged to the physically strong — the conquerors. This was followed by the era of landholders. With the arrival of the Industrial Revolution, business became the road to riches. At the same time the professions of law and medicine opened many doors to wealth.

These avenues to what is generally considered "success" still exist. But in recent decades a group once looked down upon — the court jesters — have emerged as the most highly paid and honored. So have the combatants, although professional boxers have been replaced by football players.

The entertainers — television and movie stars, singers, and comedians like Johnny Carson, Tiny Tim, the Beatles, or Elizabeth Taylor Burton — often earn far more in one year than teachers, policemen, and the others dealing with children make in a lifetime.

Another gauge of where society stands: The single most important item in many families is the automobile.

With a car the man lost in the crowd (or held down by circumstances beyond his control) can become an equal of all others on the road. He can shut out all others in the world or curse them with his horn. A car offers the feeling of power and progress—passing others by. It gives one "control" of his environment.

To a child, a car can become the symbol of growing up. Driving, like smoking and drinking, is equated with adulthood. It is not surprising, then, that thousands of children seek these things — and get into trouble. Auto theft ranks high as a cause of commitment to reform school.

Compared with war's cost

Still another way to assess how society permits delinquency to exist is in the way a nation spends its money. The Department of Commerce reports that in 1967 (latest figures available) Americans spent $36.6 billion dollars on automobiles and parts. Another $14.5 billion went for alcoholic beverages; while $9.2 billion was spent on tobacco products. Americans spend roughly $2 billion dollars a year on pets.

Yet total expenditures for the 110,000 children locked in reform schools in 1967 was only a fraction of that—an estimated $209 million, according to the Department of Health, Education, and Welfare.

That is considerably less than the cost of a week of the Vietnam war.

No accurate data is available on what is spent on juvenile probation. Nor are there figures on what is being spent for emotionally and mentally retarded children.

The federal budget for fiscal 1970 includes spending estimates of $3.9 billion for "farm-income stabilization"—which means paying farmers not to farm, crop price supports, surplus food purchases. Another $4.9 billion is expected to be spent for highway building. Defense spending will total more than $80 billion—with $27.7 billion earmarked for the Vietnam war. Several billion dollars has been earmarked for politically popular Army Corps of Engineer dams and power plants.

The Congress passed a Juvenile Delinquency and Control Act last July, and it was signed by the President on July 31. Funds totaling $5 million were authorized for fiscal 1969—obviously inadequate—but so far none of these meager funds have been released to the states.

It has been reported that the Navy will spend that much to reclaim the submarine that was accidentally sunk in dry dock in San Francisco Bay a few days ago.

Most recent figures for child-welfare services are those for the fiscal year ending June 30, 1967.

Local, state, and federal expenditures totaled an estimated $452.7 million. Of this, an estimated $283.3 million (or 63 percent) went for 283,400 children in 132,700 foster homes. And $128.3 million (28 percent) was spent on welfare department payrolls.

Not included in the total spent for child-welfare services is another $29.6 million by state and local agencies for the operation of institutions and group homes for dependent and neglected children.

One finds research is extremely skimpy — where it exists at all — in this neglected field of children in trouble.

Far more valid research has been done (and more money spent) on raising of pigs, chickens, corn, or cucumbers than on solving the problems of our troubled youth.

But as one reform-school official put it:

"Farmers have an effective lobby. Children in trouble have no one they can count on. If they had someone, they wouldn't be in trouble."

Some community answers

When parents fail and their children become a menace to society, what should be done?

The traditional answer is to channel children through the criminal process: arrest, court, inadequate or punitive probation, reform school, prison.

Yet as this series has shown, the most knowledgeable professionals in the correctional field say not only is this process self-defeating, it squanders taxpayers' money.

It can cost $8,000 a year or more to keep a child in an ineffective training school. And then too many "naughty" children return to prey on the community as hardened criminals, the experts add.

Nor, as last week's article indicated, is penalizing parents the answer.

To find the solution we must first consider why we have *organized* communities —our towns, cities, counties, states.

Organized communities exist (at least in concept) to give order to our lives and to provide a level of service and expertise that would be too costly if we tried to provide them for ourselves.

One need only imagine the cost and confusion if each citizen, with his individual tastes, interests, and ability to pay, were responsible either for contracting for paving the street in front of his house or for the construction of storm and sewer trunk lines.

The same is true of public schools, parks, or the fire department.

Careful controls set up

Perhaps the fire department is the best model for explaining how a community can come to grips with delinquency.

To begin with, much of the community emphasis is not on fighting fires. It is on fire prevention.

Local ordinances regulate installation of wiring, burning of trash, fire-retardant materials in walls and roofs, furnaces, storage of fuels and flammable materials, curbing smoking in public buildings—whatever is found to be the cause of fires. Inspectors are hired to see that laws are followed.

Meanwhile, the fire department is standing by to swing into action when preventive measures fail. The men are carefully trained. And they have a variety of tools and equipment—pumpers, snorkle units, hoses, ladders, nets, fans, inhalators, ropes, whatever is needed to do the job.

Firemen are not punitive. They punish neither the house nor the occupants, even when a fire starts through ignorance, carelessness, or violations of the law. Their interest is in stopping the fire with quick, efficient, emergency measures.

Only when there is clear evidence that the fire was deliberately set—provable arson— does the community take criminal action.

Communities also take steps to prevent delinquency.

Children must attend school until age 16; some communities impose a curfew hour; parks and playgrounds are provided; churches, mental health clinics, social organizations such as Boy Scouts and Little League provide both counseling, recreation, and positive alternatives to misbehavior.

This is enough for most children—those with the support of adequate parents living in a decent neighborhood.

But what of children with careless, selfish, ignorant, or destructive parents?

What of youngsters who live in neighborhoods where prostitution, gambling, alcoholism, ignorance, filth, poverty, stealing, and violence are the norm—where there are few or no parks, where schools are old and overcrowded, where recreation is what you find in the streets with the gang?

It is these children who fill our reform schools, mental hospitals, and other institutions.

The community fails

Like the family, the community (which is really the family enlarged) has failed.

The community fails for the same reasons the family fails—carelessness, selfishness, ignorance, poverty. And the community fails because, like the family, it can be destructive—it too often hurts instead of helps.

What does the community need to do to help children in trouble beyond the obvious preventive measures — enforcing existing housing laws; improving schools; providing more parks, lighted playgrounds, tutors, libraries, recreation leaders, and instructors and materials in arts and crafts, music, and other nondelinquent activities?

What is needed is an emergency unit, not unlike the fire department (or highway department or utility repair crew) trained and with the proper equipment, that can move in swiftly and solve problems quickly with positive rather than punitive action—solve them before they get out of control.

A child is starting to steal? Perhaps he only needs a job or some other source of spending money.

Some help for schooling

A youngster failing in school? He may need a tutor, a quiet place to study; or help in coping with a negative attitude toward education in the home. Perhaps he needs someone to show him how to get along with a poor teacher.

An angry or violent youngster? He may not have proper controls in the home. He may be going hungry or have an alcoholic father who beats him. What he needs is help —not a lecture from the police or a few days in jail.

A child wandering the streets? He may have no one to care for him. (I was surprised to find how many runaway children make an effort to be noticed by policemen—hoping to be caught and thus cared for. I was shocked to discover that much delinquent behavior is a form of crying out for help — children unable to communicate their critical needs in any other way.)

If communities are to solve these problems at least three steps must be taken:

1. Existing agencies and institutions must become more effective in dealing with children in trouble. Staffs must be better trained.

2. New services must be provided.

3. Volunteer programs must be begun or enlarged, drawing upon the many and varied talents and interests of citizens.

In the 1967 report by the President's Commission on Law Enforcement and Administration of Justice it was suggested that to en fragmentation of existing services and to reach youngsters getting no service at all:

"Communities should establish neighborhood youth-serving agencies—Youth Service Bureaus—located if possible in comprehensive neighborhood community centers and receiving juveniles (delinquents and nondelinquents) referred by the police, the juvenile court, parents, schools, and other sources."

Better use of existing agencies might include adding skilled investigators to the juvenile court staff—if the juvenile court is to remain as the keystone of this field. (Many professionals, including some with the National Council on Crime and Delinquency, urge that more and more children be channeled out of the court process.)

Whenever a child is reported to be in trouble—day or night, by police or any other agency—the investigator would be immediately sent to the home. If the home is supportive, then the child could be returned —rather than spending days, even weeks in jail or detention.

If the home is obviously damaging—immediate action could be taken toward correcting these problems by contacting existing agencies.

Beyond this, schools might remain open at night and all summer—staffed by volunteers if necessary. Courses should be offered in auto mechanics and other fields that excite youngsters.

In Minneapolis a licensed pilot has trained delinquents in navigation. As a final exam youngsters serve as navigators for pilots flying small planes to the Canadian border and back.

Some successful experiments

Policemen might be used as school counselors, as is so effectively done in some Michigan cities. Or sports stars could spend off-seasons doing community-relations work for the police, as has been the case in St. Louis.

Funds should be made available for camping trips and other outings for children who find Boys Scouts, Boys Clubs, and agencies "square"—or cannot join because they are too alienated to conform to rules and regulations.

Every community that sends three or four children to reform school or other institu-

Right goals and motives can reach the child

tions each year should build a group home. Smaller cities like Boulder, Colo. (which calls them attention homes), and Idaho Falls, Idaho (both in the 30,000 to 40,000 population range), are leading the way.

No children should be kept in jail—regardless of the size of the community. Small detention homes, to be used only for violent or self-destructive children, should be built. Each should have adequate staff and program. Welfare department shelter-care institutions and short-term-care foster homes are needed for all other children who cannot be returned to their own homes.

Young people need jobs—both after school, on weekends, and during summer vacations. Dropouts critically need employment if they are to stay out of trouble. Business groups service clubs, a housewife with business skill, a governmental or school official, even high-school or college students can run clearing houses for jobs.

On Atlanta's West Side, young people have developed a successful program called Rent-A-Kid. Youngsters babysit, mow lawns, wash windows, and do other chores.

Youngsters in trouble may need help in filling out application forms. They may need transportation, breakfast, group counseling in how to keep a job.

Older youngsters also need status. They need to be needed.

In an earlier age they had responsibilities on the farm or the family business or at home. They had a role. They felt useful. Today many have become almost like possessions—to be loved, cherished, comforted, and educated.

Some of the most exciting conversations I have had with youngsters in reform school centered around a 15-year-old relative of mine who worked as a professional carpenter's helper when his home was being remodeled. After careful instruction he roofed the entire house, then wired the addition—passing the building inspector's check. Children behind bars long for such an opportunity, I found.

Unselfed alternatives

Youngsters should be encouraged individually and in groups to make someone else's life brighter. Reading to the elderly in a nursing home; running errands for those who are incapacitated; painting houses, churches, and other buildings for the poor; and other projects help young people find themselves and feel useful.

Usually youngsters are left off local planning boards—sometimes even for teen-centers. Yet many have been known to give useful suggestions and even make the difference between a program's success and failure.

Because of the generation gap, young people who are "making it" can sometimes best reach other young people. In 1940 a young seminarian in Texas decided that since so many teen-agers turned away from formal religion, he would reach them by going where they were—the pool halls, the football field, the soda fountain.

Young Life, headed by Bill Starr, now holds meetings in living rooms in many parts of the United States and overseas.

Ten years ago Bill Milliken met a Young Life worker in a pool hall in Pittsburgh. Bill was given a free trip to a Young Life ranch in Colorado (he reports 15,000 high-school students will go to these ranches this summer).

Bill returned to Pittsburgh, attended the university there, and after two years he and his roommate, a former drug addict, decided to work with youngsters on the streets of New York's Harlem. After developing a successful program there—without funds—they moved to the lower East Side of Manhattan.

Now they are funded by the Eli Lily Foundation and from Wall Street business firms. The operating budget his year is $125,000.

In the shadow of the Brooklyn Bridge Bill and a paid staff of 24 work with drug addicts—a shocking number as young as 9 and 10—and with other children in trouble from three housing projects. Bill also trains other street workers.

At this newspaper's request, the New York State Division for Youth sent an investigator to evaluate the program. He was "very much impressed."

Women with typing skills, retired teachers, art, drama, music, and dance instructors, men and women with interest or skill in fishing, camping, writing, welding, weaving, sewing, cooking, stamp collecting, or judo Indian wrestling have something to offer.

More and more big-city youngsters receive free summer camping experiences. Farm families are taking in ghetto youngsters for a week or longer. A few middle-class couples are including deprived children when they take vacation trips.

For any volunteer program, leadership is needed. It may emerge when one concerned person telephones friends and nighbors. It may exist—in a club, service, or professional group. Or it may be sought.

Chicago shows one way

Large numbers of youngsters can be individually helped in this way. But to turn a city around, to curb the destructive elements built into a community, local government must understand the problems of children in trouble. It must recognize the causes of delinquency and combat these causes.

Cities across the nation may learn something from the experience of the Chicago Youth Development Project — a six-year joint effort of Chicago Boys Clubs and the Institute for Social Research at the University of Michigan.

The project, largest ever tried in Chicago, was financed by a $1,225,000 grant from the Ford Foundation and $174,000 from the W. Clement and Jessie B. Stone Foundation. Unlike most programs, it was backed up by careful research.

(A book "Action in the Street," will soon be published by the YMCA's Association Press. The book describes the project and its findings in detail.)

Using street-club workers who made contact with youngsters on the corners, wherever they found them, and utilizing storefront "outposts" for clubhouses (for youngsters who would not enter or were unacceptable to traditional Boys Clubs) as well as the adult meeting places, the project touched some 5,000 individuals.

During the six years (1960-1966) the staff has found 750 jobs for 490 young people; returned 950 dropouts to school 1,400 times; made 1,250 appearances at police stations and courts in behalf of 800 youngsters in which cases were either handled by station adjustment or probation; and made 2,700 follow-up visits to homes of 2,000 juveniles arrested during the last 30 months of the project.

With those individuals touched directly there was much success. But another part of the project failed. Officials had hoped to make meaningful changes in the project area—a mile and a half square with 50,000 people in it, including 4,000 young men between the ages of 10 and 19.

What they couldn't do

Writes Hans W. Mattick, one of those who ran the program:

"Despite the successful efforts of the staff in finding jobs, in returning school dropouts, and intervening in formal legal processes, the youth-employment rate remained at about the same level; the school dropout rate increased slightly; and the arrest rate in the project area increased over [a period of] time, with a lesser proportion of them being disposed of as station adjustments."

While the workers successfully helped individual youngsters with their relations with employers, the police and schools could not expand the job market; could not influence the overall behavior of youngsters and school officials in the community; could not prevent the rate of arrests from increasing.

Mr. Mattick concludes that despite a skilled staff and the expenditure of a considerable sum (two-thirds of the $1.3 million was used for the "action" portion of the project, one-third for research), the Chicago Youth Development Project's effort "apparently . . . was not sufficient to overcome the systematic production of delinquency" by the community.

The Chicago experience shows that one agency—no matter how dedicated—cannot do the job by itself. All elements of a community, public and private, must be working toward a common goal. If one agency sees its role in helping children as rehabilitative while another takes a punitive tack, the community is taking one step forward and another back at the same time.

Coordination of resources requires enlightened leadership. That kind of leadership prospers where citizens are concerned. The more people a community can involve in efforts to solve its problems, the more certain those efforts are to succeed.

Much valuable information on community programs may be obtained at low cost from:

The National Council on Crime and Delinquency, 44 East 23rd Street, New York, N.Y. 10010; the Office of Juvenile Delinquency and Youth Development, United States Department of Health, Education, and Welfare, Washington, D.C. 20201; from Children's Charter, 703 Westnedge Avenue, Kalamazoo, Mich. 49007; and from the National Congress of Parents and Teachers (PTA), 700 North Rush Street, Chicago, Ill. 60611.

An excellent booklet has also been prepared by the Ohio Youth Commission, 2280 West Broad Street, Columbus, Ohio 43223 for those living in that state.

Much useful material is also available from the New York State Division for Youth, 2 University Place, Albany, N.Y. 12203; and from the California Youth Authority, 401 State Office Building No. 1, Sacramento, Calif. 95814.

CHAPTER X

Schools don't have to make delinquents

For a few hours a day, public schools are given the task of educating children. Along with an education, however, they are called on to provide for children with special problems. Too often the schools are not geared to solve them. The result: dropouts and delinquency. The following two chapters examine the problems and explore some answers.

PUBLIC SCHOOLS TOO OFTEN UNWITtingly produce delinquents. They do this by inadequate teaching in the lower grades; by letting certain children become classroom goats; by refusing to recognize that there are both "hand" and "head" children; by believing they can punish children into learning; and by pushing youngsters with learning problems out of school.

In this newspaper's study it was found that nationally court commitments to reform school drop sharply in the summer months.

Commitments begin to climb when schools open in the fall, peaking in November or December, then tapering off, only to peak again in the spring.

It has often been pointed out in this series that children are in trouble for a variety of reasons. It is significant, however, that in at least 80 percent of all cases taken to court, one can find that a school problem was an important factor.

Teachers know this. At least the more thoughtful teachers do. Warnings appear regularly in a student's records. But too often nothing is done about it until the child is in serious trouble.

Robert is a tall, 15-year-old Negro from Brooklyn. I found him swinging an ax at a New York Division for Youth forest camp near Ithaca.

Home instruction advised

At age 4 Robert had lead poisoning from eating paint in a slum apartment. He never knew his father. His mother worked. The home was a mess. He seldom got proper

meals. He wet his pants until he was 12, and he had a speech defect. When he skipped school, as he often did, he spent the day alone in the apartment.

In June, 1960, one teacher wrote on his record: "Robert needs very patient handling and affection and then he is an ideal pupil. Otherwise he tends to withdraw himself and seems very unhappy."

In February, 1961, another teacher wrote: "Reading is a task he has not mastered." A month later she added: "Robert seems to be very unhappy. He is alone with his thoughts and the beating of his heart. He is unable to adjust to a classroom situation. He did not do any academic work."

Because Robert could not adapt, the report shows, "the Bureau of Child Guidance made referral for home instruction in 1963, but it was never acted upon."

Robert by now was skipping school regularly. In April, 1964, his teacher wrote: "Unhappy, disinterested child, truant." In May, 1965, the teacher only noted: "Persistently truant."

Then Robert did not return to school the following fall. During the next two years he "sat around home, watched TV, looked out of the window, wandered around the neighborhood." Yet he did not steal or otherwise get in trouble with the police.

Lecture falls short

When he was finally taken to court by an attendance officer he received a lecture and some threats from the judge. But nothing happened. He was hauled into court again and put on probation.

An "I-care-about-you" approach

The New York City Probation Department is understaffed, overworked, lacks enough talented manpower, and is generally ineffective. Again nothing happened.

Probation ran out. He was returned to court and put on probation again. Still there was no change.

In February, 1968, after another session in court, Robert listened to the judge's threats, then returned to school briefly. The records show that, though he could read only at the first-grade level and had been out of school two years, he was placed in the eighth grade. He stayed only a few days.

In late April he was back in court. The judge then wrote: "I again defer placement [in an institution] in view of the board of education's statement that home instruction can probably be accomplished in three or four weeks."

Again, the school system failed to keep its promise.

Then summer came. That was followed by a teachers' strike.

But when the strike ended and Robert still did not go to school, he was returned to court. Then he was sent to the forest camp—perhaps the best thing that ever happened to him.

A year in four months

"I like school here," he told me. "My reading was very bad when I came. I read a little better now. But not good enough. I like the teachers a lot better here. On the outside [back in Brooklyn] they got on my nerves. They keep shoutin' at you. Here they help you."

This, then, is the second significant finding in this newspaper's study of schools and children in trouble: Not only can youngsters given up by the public schools learn—often progressing as much as one or two years in a few months in the right setting—but they *like* school.

At the Los Guilucos School for Girls near Santa Rosa, Calif., the goal of the reading laboratory is to advance a student one academic year in four months. A 16-year-old Negro girl from San Francisco I met at the school had been reading at the fifth-grade level when she arrived six months earlier. Now she was handling seventh-grade material.

At the Maryland School for Boys, six 15-year-olds who could not read at all when they arrived were making headway only a few months after the new reading lab opened in September.

"Man, if they had this stuff [equipment] at the outside school [in Baltimore] I wouldn't mind goin'," one of them told me as he worked with a tape recorder.

A touch of 'I care'

Equipment and small classes help, but they are not enough. It takes exceptional teachers to reach children in trouble. And there are too few exceptional teachers available.

This leads to a third point of special interest discovered in this newspaper's study: Almost all teachers who succeeded in reaching children in trouble shunned traditional lectures so common in the typical classroom.

Almost all worked in small groups. And some touched the children from time to time — touched them on the hand, the wrist, the arm or shoulder in an "I-care-about-you" manner not unlike the football coach as he discusses a crucial play with a star quarterback. A few succeed in communicating without touching by skillfully and probably unconsciously using very expressive eyes.

At Public School 148 in New York, a "special school for socially maladjusted and emotionally disturbed children," I watched teachers scream and stamp their feet, even hit a child. But the one teacher who was getting through, Miss Flora Boyd, gathered desks into small groups and controlled youngsters by gently touching them. When she graded work she put an arm around the child's shoulder — lightly, naturally.

Closeness without contact

A few days later I visited PS 82, another special school on the lower East Side. In one room I found students huddled around a small table, shoulders touching. In the next they were tightly grouped at the blackboard. In each room teachers worked closely with the students. In each room students were learning!

I asked the principal about this. Joseph P. Del Barto, a clinical psychologist who has specialized in reading, said he does not allow his teachers to touch the children. But he carefully trains all teachers to work in small, intimate groups. In his 20 years' working with children he had found it the best way to reach them.

Wherever I went I found that where children in trouble were learning, the teacher had developed some form of special, warm, intimate relationship with the youngsters.

In effect, such a teacher supplies the child with what sociologists call a "primary group" relationship — the warmth and love normally provided by the family and close friends.

Homelike expectations

Dr. Eloise C. Snyder, professor of sociology at Columbia College in Columbia, S.C., is studying the problems of delinquents. She believes that many of these children expect members of their "secondary groups" (teachers, policemen, bus drivers, store clerks, etc.) to act like those in their primary group.

When a teacher, for example, responds to a child in "normal" secondary-group fashion and fails to form an intimate relationship, the youngster sees this as hostility or rejection.

This is in keeping with Dr. Rita Warren's I-level (interpersonal relationship) study, discussed earlier in this series. Dr. Warren, researcher for the California Youth Commission, found that a large number of delinquents are immature. Even in their teens these youngsters may relate to others in the same way small children do—searching for attention, support, love.

Interviews with children and an examination of reports prepared by social workers around the country indicate that most delinquents come from homes lacking these qualities—homes that are really secondary, rather than primary groups.

Varied responses stressed

In California delinquency programs, certain groups of children—those classified as I-3 (immature conformists)—respond quickly to the very supportive, gentle worker. This often results in early discharge from institutions or probation, since progress is so often gauged by conformity.

But the failure rate of these children has been high. They could not cope alone. Encouraged to join the Army because officials thought it to be "supportive," many of these boys went absent without leave or otherwise failed. (The Army would be classified as a secondary group.)

It was concluded that it was a serious mistake to release these youngsters and that a long-term program (involving a primary relationship) was needed until they "grew up." This, Dr. Warren says, has been effective.

It should also be pointed out that Dr. Warren and her coworkers in California have found that certain children do not respond well to an intimate or touching relationship—especially those classified as more mature but somewhat neurotic.

Dr. Warren emphasizes that children do not all respond to a person in the same way. And the opposite is also true. Thus the importance of carefully matching children with staff.

Schools with children who do not learn to read, for example, could quickly find out (a) if the child responds best in a primary or secondary group and (b) if there is a personality barrier between teacher and pupil. If the child needs an intimate (primary) group, or if his teacher is intolerant of his behavior and there is a clash, then changes should be made. (This screening would better take place prior to assigning the child to a teacher.)

What happens in the schools is not too different from the "natural" screening that may take place between employer and worker—who is either fired or transferred when there is a continuing clash. Except with pupils it is called "expulsion."

Understanding the matching process and the primary- and secondary-group concept also should prove of value to others dealing with young people.

Today more and more people accept the thesis that when children do not learn, it is the fault of the school or the teacher, not of the child.

Diverse tasks assigned

Yet school officials say they are being handed an impossible task: In 5 or 6 hours a day they are being asked to tackle problems which the family, church, and community have failed to solve. Educators are being asked to compensate for fractured homes, poverty, slums, stupidity, greed, and all the other environmental flaws that contribute to delinquency.

These new tasks being handed to the schools involve such diverse areas as sex education, the hiring of school social workers to deal with home problems, school dental and medical clinics, staff psychologists and psychiatrists, career counselors, free or low-cost breakfasts and lunches in schools, homemaking classes, and emphasis on such things as "socialization" (essentially, learning to get along in the group).

As schools take more and more responsibility for the child, two things appear to be happening:

1. The breakdown of the family is accelerated. Parents find themselves either left behind or in conflict with what is being taught in the schools.

2. The schools are diverted from their primary goal: teaching children certain basic skills that will enable the youngsters to make their way in the world.

School systems are heavily weighted with curriculum coordinators, counselors, administrators, and a variety of specialists who prod bright youngsters on their way to college. Yet in most schools there are youngsters who cannot read (at least at grade level), cannot write, and find it difficult to do simple arithmetic and impossible to find a decent job when they leave school.

Basic variation unheeded

Psychologists complain that too few schools recognize that there are what have been called "head" children and "hand" children.

A head child is one who deals easily with abstractions — with theories, concepts, ideas. Or he may be able to memorize words from a book.

A hand child is the youngster who is more practical, often more physically active, more concerned with immediate rewards, more caught up in material things than in vague concepts.

This newspaper's study shows that the hand child is more often the one in trouble. He may enter school without having held a book, magazine, or newspaper. He has little concept of communicating ideas. Immature, he wants what he wants now, not later. And what he wants more often satisfies a physical need.

This is why he is easily manipulated by behaviorists, who have discovered one way to get such a child to learn is to pay him—either with money, candy, or something else he wants. They motivate him with immediate physical gratification. Delayed rewards —like a high mark on his report card or his name on the honor roll every few weeks—don't provide him with any meaningful payoff.

Such a child usually responds to the attention he gets in an intimate primary group, but a large class turns him off.

Vocational schools added

Because he gets pleasure from things rather than thinking, he enjoys working with his hands and in "doing." Because a car may represent so many things to him—achieving adult status, freedom from parental supervision, power, control of his environment for the first time, status he has never had—having one may become an obsession. He may steal a car, or drop out of school to buy one to satisfy this hunger.

What this boy needs is a vocational school. More are being built across the country. Helena, Mont., has recently opened an excellent facility, for example. The Job Corps, too, has been filling the gap. Camp Breckenridge in Kentucky is doing a first-rate job of training youngsters. Many prisons and some reform schools are also offering strong vocational programs. One of the best is at Rikers Island in New York.

But children in trouble should not automatically be shunted into a vocational school.

Many of those children are imaginative, creative. But these qualities have been channeled into delinquent acts rather than into school. Thus children who might make important contributions to society are excluded from high school or college and work at a job that bores them. Instead youngsters who can sit still and feed back answers like robots have a much better chance of succeeding in society.

Problem boy in 'ideal' system

What can happen to the hand child?

Joe is a husky, 15-year-old hand child. He lives in Greeley, Colo., a delightful college town of 34,000 some 50 miles north of Denver.

The chamber of commerce boasts of Greeley's many qualities in a nicely boxed collection of brochures in bright covers: abundant sunshine, low humidity, 10 public parks, adult band, three golf courses, skiing, mountain climbing, fishing, swimming pool, college and professional football, horse racing, dog racing, stock-car racing and other sports in town or within an hour's drive, an excellent labor market, good newspapers, radio, television, transportation, utilities, council-manager government, 36 full-time policemen, 31 full-time firemen with a 75-foot snorkel unit, plenty of drinking water, an economy based on agriculture.

No one talks about Joe

Early settlers coined the slogan "Things Grow Better in Greeley," and the chamber of commerce unblushingly says this is a fact.

One segment of its school system—an all-boy kindergarten and first grade with male teachers—has been written up in national publications.

But no one talks about Joe. This summer he turns 16, and it is doubtful he will return to school in the fall. As in so many other cities, between a quarter and a third of the Greeley students drop out of school.

Joe has been known to Charles M. Smith, the thoughtful, concerned assistant director of pupil personnel, for five years. He has tried to help Joe—even referring him to a mental-health clinic for psychiatric care. (The psychiatrist reported back that Joe's mother, after a few visits, stopped taking him; and, he told Mr. Smith, it is the mother, not Joe, who really needs treatment.)

Even before Mr. Smith met him, Joe had been a school problem. In elementary school he was placed in a remedial-reading class. He was given more remedial reading in junior high. He was also placed in a speech and hearing clinic because his mother insisted he was deaf in one ear. Joe says it is the other ear. And a physician insists Joe's hearing is normal.

Teacher threatened

Like so many other children this reporter has seen, Joe was not the best pupil in elementary school, but having only one teacher, he was able to survive. Then, as he progressed through junior high and high school he had different teachers during the day. Each year he became more of a problem—eventually threatening a teacher, shoving, hitting back when he was hit.

During his school career perhaps 50 professionals have dealt with Joe—teachers, administrators, social workers, psychologists—each with his own theory and in his own way.

This has ranged from one extreme to another—from aggressive discipline with a paddle by a vice-principal to the permissive "poor Joe" approach—often on the same day.

Descriptions vary

Nor did all teachers see him as the same boy. This depended on the teacher's approach (primary or secondary group), personality (tolerance of a child with Joe's traits), subject matter (dull or interesting to Joe), and peer-group response.

When his six teachers sat down together to discuss Joe and his problems, their descriptions of him swung from "passive" and "does nothing" to "hostile," "violent,"

and "I expect him to be a murderer some day."

While Joe is battered from pillar to post at school, he has little help at home. Neither his mother, his father (a construction worker), nor his older sister finished high school.

Yet Joe can do things with his hands. Mr. Smith has found that he (and many of the youngsters like him) can communicate, can learn in an intimate (primary) relationship away from the school.

Greeley cannot really be blamed for what has happened to Joe, in that it has a better-than-average school system and it is doing what most schools do.

Yet perhaps this is really not an excuse. Greeley has found the money to equip and ship a handful of boys around the state to play football and basketball. It has fine streets, 10 parks, public buildings, and all of the other things listed in the chamber brochure. It has school officials with enough imagination to start the all-boy kindergarten because it is believed small boys need activity and a male environment in which to learn.

This newspaper found in its visit to more than 40 states that there are tens of thousands of children in trouble because the schools have failed to meet their needs. And, as in Joe's case, their parents have often failed, too.

The nation's prisons and reform schools are full of these failures. Yet this society is willing to pay $8,000 a year or more to keep a child in an inadequate, punitive institution while spending only a few hundred dollars a year for his education while he lives at home.

How to salvage the dropouts

Scattered here and there across the country are impressive new school programs designed to help children in trouble.

In Burlington, Vt., Project Aspire has just completed its third year.

Ten to 20 students in trouble—dropouts or potential dropouts—are taught by two exceptional teachers, Charles (Chick) Ash and Leo Le Cours.

The day I was there students had been out on the shore of Lake Champlain gathering moss, lichens, and other plants for a science project. While there, they found a family of mice in a hollow log. These were placed in a terrarium. Suddenly these active hand children were opening books to learn about their find.

The guitar-playing Mr. Le Cours teaches English, social studies, and music by having

the youngsters write historical folk ballads to be sung in class.

When the project first started and was funded by the federal government, the class studied the Everglades by buying tickets and flying to Florida to see them. (This expensive part of the program has been discontinued.)

Model of a 'Sopwith Camel'

This year youngsters have been building a full-scale model of Snoopy's "Sopwith Camel"—a biplane depicted in the popular "Peanuts" comic strip.

Both teachers admit they "changed as much as the kids" during the first year —and Aspire has made them far more effective as teachers. But it was found that

many youngsters who suddenly blossomed under Messrs. Ash and Le Cours began to fail again when, the following year, they were returned to the traditional classroom. (To understand why, see discussion of primary and secondary groups in preceding article.)

To bridge this gap two more "warm, sympathetic" teachers were picked to help ease Aspire students back into the mainstream.

More important, says principal Glenn M. Fay, the other teachers in the system began to see how effective the new approach could be. He says that Burlington High School has changed and that fewer teachers are worried about their status and rigid professional role.

"More are working with kids, if not as equals, at least as real human beings," he says.

Seattle work-study setup

In Seattle I found another hopeful program—Project Interchange. In an old building once used for dependent and delinquent youngsters, school dropouts and other boys in trouble go to class five hours a day, then spend the rest of the day in nursing homes, a school forest, or other vocational and work programs.

Project Interchange, a work-study program, is funded by the Job Corps in co-operation with the Seattle public schools. But, unlike the traditional Job Corps centers (some of them frightening places with many of the shortcomings of reform schools, and where I found white youngsters often have been driven away because of physical attacks by black student trainees), Project Interchange keeps the boys at home.

The academic program includes emphasis on remedial reading and math. But since the first of the year it has been broadened to include science, health, language arts, and social studies. Programmed learning with individual instruction is used. There is no limit to the time a student may take— fast or slow, he works at his own speed.

Ten boys are involved in a graphic arts course—taught in a high school after regular students leave for the day. A half-dozen others go to two nursing homes where they serve trays, help people into bed and wheelchairs, give baths, take guests on walks, and just cheer them up by talking.

Still others landscape the grounds of the school, paint, clean, and learn to do other maintenance jobs. Some work in the school snack bar, while others are in training to work in gas stations. About a dozen go to the Cleveland High School Memorial Forest, where they are building a nature trail

and shelters. (Students are paid $1.60 an hour.)

Emphasis, says Richard Case, the center director, is not only on academic subjects and work skills but also on counseling.

"If we can build their self-confidence, give them greater insight into themselves and help them establish goals, then the other comes easily," he says.

Funding in danger

Like so many experimental programs, the project is in danger on two fronts. Funding runs out June 30, and the Nixon administration is clipping off large chunks of the Job Corps nationally. (Project Interchange costs roughly $1,800 per student per year, only a fraction of the cost of the traditional live-in Job Corps center—$8,000 per youngster per year.)

Typical neighborhood pressure on the school board is driving the project from its present location. Located in a white, middle-class area, it draws complaints from those who live around the school. They say youngsters cut across their lawns, sometimes use offensive language, and wander around in the neighborhood. So far no new location has been found.

Starting with 50 youngsters, Project Interchange was recently enlarged to 135. Yet between 1,500 and 2,000 young people drop out of school in Seattle each year.

Unusual staff in New Mexico

In Albuquerque, N.M., I visited the Esperanza School. Translated, esperanza means "hope," and that is what the school offers children in trouble, many of them from Mexican-American backgrounds.

Roughly 100 boys doing work in grades 1 to 11, reading 2 to 6 years below their grade level, are being helped, says Eddie Castillo, who heads the school. Four unusual teachers have been selected at this school.

One, Jack Williams, has a Ph.D. in administration. Another, Charles Groffman, has a degree in anthropology and has traveled abroad widely. Earl Johnson is a retired Army colonel. Betty Starkey taught in a traditional classroom for 10 years, then worked with dropouts in a federal manpower-development program.

Mr. Groffman's colleagues call him "fantastic." I found his students excited about learning and making surprising progress.

Classes are held in old World War II officer quarters and two metal "portable classrooms." While both traditional teaching methods and programmed learning are used, each teacher is permitted to employ the technique he finds most effective.

Skills for earning

A quarter of the boys have been referred to the school by the juvenile court; roughly 43 percent were sent because they were failing in the public schools; 15 percent came because they or their parents asked that they be admitted; 7.5 percent were in the program, went back to the regular school, and have returned; while not quite 10 percent were referred by welfare officials.

Exciting high school

One of the nation's most exciting high schools can be found in the tiny peach-growing community of Hughson, Calif., out in the warm San Joaquin Valley 100 miles east of San Francisco. In 1959 Hughson Union High School barely passed state accreditation. Lacking a librarian, with inadequate science equipment and materials, with a poor program for students not going to college, and with several other flaws, it was typical of many high schools in rural areas.

Today hundreds of educators from California and other parts of the nation visit Hughson: Its faculty is training other California teachers; and the school is being used as a model for those in other communities.

It began with the determination to "do it better" than traditional schools. This led Hughson officials to study other California schools. It eventually led them to the highly regarded Nova schools in Fort Lauderdale. Fla.

Nova agreed to serve as a "mother school," training Hughson's teachers and offering advice.

With a three-year, $357,000 federal grant and the help of his teachers and school board, Robert R. Reeder (who arrived in Hughson in 1947 to teach social studies and in 1960 became superintendent) made drastic changes.

It is hard to describe Hughson Union High, because it is so different from what most people are familiar with. Only the buildings are typical—though even these have such modern features as flexible walls that alter the size of the classroom as students come and go.

23 options in senior English

Hughson officials call their program "con-·tinuous-progress education." While it vaguely resembles programmed learning, it might best be compared with the traditional Boy Scout merit-badge program in that students perform a series of learning tasks at their own speed. When these tasks have been successfully completed they have earned their grade.

Mr. Reeder holds that many children have trouble in traditional schools for two reasons: frustration and boredom.

"Some kids are given assignments they can't handle, while others are being held back."

The Hughson student is given a number of options. To pass senior English, for example, students have 23 possible areas of study, but they choose only 8.

These are called learning activity packages, or LAPs.

Each LAP is written expressly for the school in sassy language that will appeal to young people. It is run off on special printing equipment and packaged in booklet form.

Each LAP begins with the "rationale"—that is, an explanation of why the student should learn what he is about to learn. After further explanations and a discussion of what the student is expected to achieve if he is to complete the LAP, he is then given the opportunity to take a test if he feels he already knows the material.

If he does not do this, then he completes a series of activities—some required, some optional. The day I was there students studying fables in an English-literature class had adapted one to perform as a play. Other students in the same class were working on other subjects they found more interesting.

Testing when ready

It is up to the student to decide when he has mastered a LAP and is ready to take the test. If he fails the test, then he studies areas where he is weak and takes the test again when he knows the material.

It is almost impossible for a student to fail a subject, since he is permitted to repeat immediately. In the traditional high school he would have to wait a year and take the entire course over.

Equally important, the teacher who once spent his full time lecturing to a class now works with individuals or small groups either in a classroom, the library, or out on the patio. He thus becomes more effective as a teacher.

For those with special problems there is a remedial-reading laboratory.

The school also has modern equipment—including a language lab run by a skilled linguist, Tomy Loomis, a graduate of Principia College, Elsah, Ill. Mr. Loomis uses recording equipment to teach several languages at once and at several levels. Students were learning Spanish, Portuguese, German, Hebrew, and Italian the day I was there.

Translation counts twice

In another innovation, students were using a natural-science textbook from Venezuela, translating it, and getting credit not only in Spanish but in their science course as well.

A student may earn two years' credit in one, or only a quarter- or half-year's credit —depending on his ability and interest.

Much progress has been made in vocational education.

"The school was college-prep oriented," Mr. Reeder says.

"We had no vocational shop facilities, not even a typewriter under 10 years old, and yet 70 percent of our students did not go on to college."

Now several vocational programs are offered.

Eighth-grade students—boys and girls—are brought in from the junior high to study art, drafting, electronics, and either home economics or wood shop. These subjects are also required in the ninth grade. All students take a semester of typing.

One exciting aspect is community involvement. The chemistry lab and other classrooms are open at night, with parents chaperoning. Parent volunteers also help out during the day, typing, proctoring tests, and freeing teachers from other mundane chores. Those with special skills may even help teach.

Cordie Qualle, the school-board president, who runs a construction company, says that for the first time "adults feel part of the school—they feel wanted."

What does this mean to children in trouble?

Self-reliance stimulated

Many problems have been solved at Hughson. Jerry Carpenter, curriculum coordinator, reports a marked drop in student vandalism, broken windows, kicked-in lockers, and other minor incidents common to most schools. Fights have stopped and students have even established their own dress code.

The improvements can be traced to a system that stimulates self-reliance: Students work at their own speed, finding it almost impossible to fail. They are given the opportunity to choose from a variety of interesting materials. They know exactly what is expected of them. Each can develop his individual talents. And, perhaps most important, one-to-one help from teachers is available when needed.

Another major dividend: The dropout rate, which averaged between 20 and 30 a year, has been reduced to zero in the past two years.

It is too early to know if this trend will continue. But it is significant that last year 13 dropouts returned to graduate—a few of them parents sitting in class with their children.

"Give me your tired, your poor,
your huddled masses yearning..."

CHAPTER XI

How fair to a child?

The child from a home receiving welfare money often
ends up behind bars. A statistic in the welfare population, he is
allocated dollars, but no real help with the personal or
environmental problems that may send him to prison. Many
experts feel the whole welfare concept needs an overhaul.
This chapter examines the flaws in the present system
and suggests new approaches.

MARILYN, 14, WAS DEEPLY DE-pressed.

It had been mid-August when she and her 16-year-old brother were picked up by police. Both had been living in a mobile home where their father, a retired Army sergeant, had abandoned them. The police had hauled the youngsters off to the Phoenix detention center — a crowded, shabby jail for children.

The court found Marilyn to be dependent and turned her over to the welfare department. Two months later she was still in detention. In those two months a caseworker had visited Marilyn only once. Now that caseworker was on vacation and could not be reached.

Eventually the police found her mother, an alcoholic, in a saloon. She was in no condition to care for her children. Nor did she have a right to take them, for the judge had given them to their father during a divorce some months before.

"Dad was never home," Marilyn says. "And when he did come home he was drunk. About two weeks before he left he caught me with a boy. He beat me and threw my boy friend and my brother's girl friend out.

"Then one day me and my brother were sittin' in the living room and Dad said, 'I'm gonna take off—if I don't I'll go crazy.' He got his clothes and gave us each $5 and left. Somebody called the police. I been here ever since."

Girl's ranch suggested

While Marilyn was locked up, Mrs. Hazel Bell, a concerned probation officer, kept calling the welfare department.

"I know its hard to find a foster home for a teen-age girl like Marilyn," Mrs. Bell says. "I suggested that they place her at a girl's ranch. Just before [the welfare worker] went on vacation she said she would try."

At least Marilyn was getting dental care —paid for by welfare. A very plain girl with a poor complexion, Marilyn was especially ashamed of her teeth.

Alan Margolin, state director of the Arizona Division of Child Welfare, at first denied that children were being locked up by his department for two months or more. Later he called it a "communications breakdown," explaining that he had ordered dependent and neglected children removed from detention.

He also complained that the Arizona Welfare Department has neither enough money, proper facilities, nor staff to care for children in trouble—especially those who have had contact with police. Many, he said, were being found delinquent in court just to have a place to put them.

"We had a four-year-old boy who was committed to the state as a delinquent," he says. "He needed help, and it was the only way we could get services."

This four-year-old was the youngest "delinquent" child found in this newspaper's study. But thousands of other youngsters have been locked up across the nation because welfare departments have nowhere to send them.

Welfare departments have dual roles: One set of social workers hands out money, then plays "policeman" checking on people who are given doles. (This is slowly changing.) Other social workers are assigned to protect and assist children through child-care ser-

A promise unfulfilled for too many children

vices. Too often the money hand doesn't know what the child-care hand is doing.

Widespread lack of funds

Child care has long been the province of private agencies—usually church sponsored. But these agencies lack funds, staff, and other means to deal with problems of the magnitude found in our nation today.

Sponsoring churches are having their own struggles. Beyond this, it is often pointed out that Protestants have never provided services to children on the scale offered by Roman Catholics and Jews. Especially neglected are Negro children.

Nor have public child-care agencies been able to do the job. While almost all of the case workers assigned are compassionate, concerned, dedicated, they lack the means to help children. Facing an extremely critical shortage of foster homes and with almost no way to upgrade existing homes, they tend to function as placement people—searching for openings in the overpacked private child-care facilities.

The money hand of welfare—the division that gives out money—tends to perpetuate poverty instead of end it. At best a welfare dole offers little more than survival—enough money to keep you from starving; a little clothing to protect you from the weather; grim shelter so that you do not have to sleep in doorways.

Public welfare is a promise that has not been kept. People flounder in squalor generation after generation. Many, interviews show, see themselves as worthless, unwanted, defeated. This feeling is quickly absorbed by the children of poverty. And these are the children who too often end up in jail, reform school, or prison.

What about taxpayers?

Many American taxpayers seem not to understand this. They are too busy being angry at welfare mothers to give much thought to children in trouble.

Too few people seem to realize that large numbers of women on welfare were themselves deprived and damaged as children; that they have been abandoned by the men who fathered their youngsters; and that little girls growing up in welfare homes may soon draw welfare checks of their own because large numbers have babies in their early teens.

Little attention is paid to the boys who sire these children — young men from the middle class as well as welfare families—"sowing wild oats." Few of these boys are old enough, or well educated enough, to support their offspring—even if someone held them responsible.

This writer found welfare children are

fed, half-clothed, more or less housed, but too seldom helped. And frustrated welfare workers are first to acknowledge this as they fight their way through governmental paperwork and red tape.

These children in trouble live in the shadow of the myths believed by taxpayers who do not understand—citizens who seem unaware that billions of tax dollars go for war spending; soaring educational costs; highway building; a wide variety of projects and "needs," created by public demand; pork-barreling by politicians who know spending tax dollars will get them reelected; and the ballooning federal bureaucracy.

In one year the United States spends $28.8 billion on the Vietnam war—enough to support AFDC (Aid to Families with Dependent Children) for 11 years.

Myths hard to pin down

It is difficult to pin down the myths that have sprung up; harder to convince those who believe them that they are mistaken. Myths that scheming women produce illegitimate children so they can make enough profit to buy luxuries like color television. Or that able-bodied men sit home waiting for the mailman to bring them welfare checks.

One who visits welfare homes finds little evidence to back up these myths—perhaps two or three examples out of a thousand cases studied.

Some officials trace the stories back to memories of programs run during the depression days of the 1930's. Others say there is confusion over welfare and payments for unemployment compensation, social security, medicare, and medicaid.

A spokesman for the Massachusetts Public Welfare Department explains that in some instances people with "some means" have received assistance with medical bills since medicaid went into effect in June of 1967. He tells of a man who received a kidney transplant costing $15,000. The man was able to "pay about half the bill, while medicaid paid the rest."

There are few able-bodied men on welfare. Men who get doles are usually blind, disabled, or aged.

Edmund McCarthy, a Massachusetts welfare official, tells of how, when he was a welfare supervisor in Lynn, Mass., he was asked by city officials to comb the general-assistance roles for men to help clean streets in the spring.

There were 200 men and women on general assistance in that community of more than 90,000 people. Checking each case he found only three men who could work—one a part-time college student who should have received assistance from some other agency, and two men who "were just about capable of following instructions to sweep streets."

All of the other men either had physical problems or were in work or training programs, including a group of alcoholics.

Nor is welfare a program solely for Negroes. The majority on welfare are white.

A federal study shows that there are roughly 9 million white children classified as "poor" in the United States. This compared with 6 million young poverty-stricken Negroes, Indians, Mexican Americans, Puerto Ricans, and members of other minority groups.

Of these 15,000,000 poor children, a total of 4,646,000 receive AFDC grants. Another 1,569,000 on AFDC are adults—the vast majority mothers. A few are unemployed fathers.

Can welfare mothers afford color television?

In California a typical welfare mother has two or three children. Her AFDC grant is roughly $176 a month. Yet a United States Department of Labor study indicates that a family of that size in Los Angeles needs roughly $350 to $400 a month to live at what is best described as a very low but decent standard of living.

State allowances vary

The typical AFDC mother in New York gets about $249 a month; in Illinois $213; in Michigan $191; in Texas $87; and in Alabama $64. Each state is different—with different standards very loosely tied to some basic federal guidelines.

And yet the Labor Department suggests that in New York City, Detroit, or Chicago a family probably needs between $300 and $400 to live at a low level; in Texas and other parts of the South the minimum amount is perhaps closer to $300 for those living in cities.

What of the larger family?

A mother in Massachusetts gets about $6.75 a week extra for each child under the age of seven—less than $1 a day. For those 7 to 12, she gets less than $10 a week; and for those between the ages of 13 and 20 she gets roughly $12 a week. That is to cover all expenses—food, shelter, furniture, clothing, school money (medical costs are not included).

Some states provide slightly more but most pay less, with Mississippi, Alabama, and Texas providing only a few cents a day.

Most citizen complaints come from people who "know someone" who saw a welfare mother cashing a check in a supermarket. To the woman running a cash register for $60 or $70 a week, a check from a woman with a large family can seem huge. A woman with a dozen children in the states in the higher range may receive a monthly dole of $500 and more. Yet based on subsistence standards, most welfare mothers receive less than they need.

Complaints—and demands

Those who complain about welfare doles also demand that welfare mothers be as good or even better money managers than typical housewives. This, of course, is not realistic.

Further, I found prices in slum stores higher than in middle-class neighborhoods. And women on welfare must too often deal with "easy-credit" shylocks for major purchases. Many pay double or triple fair-market value for shoddy furniture that will fall apart before the last payment is made. (These stores are often the first targets in a riot.)

Many welfare mothers behave in a manner unacceptable to middle-class society—which expects them not only to be exceptional money managers, but to be extremely virtuous. Some welfare mothers drink heavily. Others have casual affairs with men. These women live in ways not too different from that depicted on the afternoon television soap operas — except that welfare mothers live at the poverty level, rather than in middle-class homes.

One cannot condone this behavior in the poor any more than it should be approved of in the middle class. But listening to welfare mothers talk at least helps one understand why they behave as they do. For they are a product of their environment.

"It's common to have a man to help supplement the income," says Sherron Cleveland, a welfare mother and president of the Citizens Advisory Board for a welfare office on the west side of Chicago. "Maybe for months you eat nothin' but beans, and you decide you want a little bottle of perfume or some toothpaste. Along comes some man who says, 'I like you, how about my coming to see you.' So you let him because he'll bring you something nice.

"He may come over just once, or you may see him a few times a week for a year or two. I could name 20 welfare mothers I know, and 17 are having sex with one man, or more than one. They're searching for love, companionship— the things any woman wants.

"And if your children are going hungry— and a lot of children are here—well, I guess if you're a real mother you'll do almost anything to put food in their mouths."

Outside her window it was bedlam—children without a proper place to play — screaming, fighting, throwing stones.

"I want to go to work," she says. "When I'm home I'm irritable—I can't seem to help my children. But I'm forced to stay home because there's nobody to take care of my children. If I could get out and work, when I came home at night I'd feel like helping my kids. I can't stand this," she said gesturing at the neighborhood, the noise, the confusion, the squalor.

'You got to get away'

A neighbor who has dropped in gives her views.

"You don't have cleanser to do house-cleaning right. We know how to clean houses—we been doin' it for you people [whites] long enough. But I reach for cleanser in a store and I know I'm takin' food out of my baby's mouth, and I got to decide which child won't get fed.

"A mother's got to get away from her broken-down apartment with the rats and roaches. A welfare mother gets so little she can't give her kids the things the kids next door get. You get tired of giving them hand-me-down shoes. You have all you can take of rats and roaches and kids, and you go find a man who'll buy you something to drink.

"What goes on here affects everything you do. It affects your mind. You can't think straight when you live like this, and if you don't want to go crazy you gotta get outa here, so you find some man. What we really need is good jobs and day-care centers."

Mrs. Cleveland is excited now.

"Even if you didn't want to work, maybe you need an hour without all the crying and yelling—an hour just to sit in a bathtub and feel like a woman.

"But if we had a proper center it would have to be a place where you don't just leave the kids. It should be a place where they learn something."

These are the things welfare mothers want for their children: day-care centers with education for preschoolers; good schools; job opportunities; a decent place to live; a place for youngsters to go other than on street corners. The same things any mother wants.

David L. Daniel, who heads the Cook County Department of Public Aid, says a few days ago his office asked women on AFDC if they were willing to work. Of 4,400 replies, some 2,500 mothers said they could solve their child-care problems themselves and that they wanted to go to work.

Need for jobs discussed

Mr. Daniel's office invited in Chicago businessmen to discuss the need for jobs for welfare mothers. The 34 firms that came to the meeting pledged 500 jobs—often including job training. When welfare officials sent in 300 job orders these firms hired 200 women.

He suggests that finding work for welfare mothers may be one answer to breaking the cycle of poverty. Yet proper facilities for children while the mother works are essential, he adds. Many who say they have places for their children to go would leave the youngsters "with a neighbor, an old grandma, or an immature baby sitter." And a major reason for welfare mothers to quit work is the failure of child care to work out," he adds.

While mothers working may solve some problems, new ones are created. As has been pointed out in this series, many children in trouble have gotten in trouble in their own homes when the mother is out. And youngsters wandering the streets are the most delinquency prone.

Rural problems are not too different from those of the city—except that there is more fresh air and play space for children.

Mrs. Evelyn Smith is a welfare worker in Rock Springs, Wyo. She finds white women the hardest to reach because they are "functioning just enough to stay out of the mental hospital."

"I've worked in three counties," she says. "The few Negroes we have still have desires and wants and are willing to fight for them. The Spanish Americans know they will make it. But the whites are really at the bottom. Many live on the fringes of towns, and they are almost completely invisible. Some whites don't react at all when you go into their homes—they don't even get angry. They are completely flat."

I discovered the poor behave in very similar ways regardless of race. Mrs. Smith finds the same things in Wyoming that I observed in every state I visited.

Families on welfare—especially whites—have an "overwhelming feeling of insecurity—a feeling of inadequacy of their own personality," she says. "They find it difficult to relate to other people meaningfully."

Homes miserable

Most of the homes are "miserable," she adds. The women usually "act out sexually—sometimes sleeping with whatever man is interested." And they "pass their problems on to their daughters."

It is clear that money really isn't the whole answer to families in trouble. This is why the guaranteed annual wage—presently being considered by the Nixon administration—will not alone solve the welfare problem.

Most welfare officials agree with this. But

they add that with a guaranteed annual wage they would have more time to resolve their clients' deep-rooted problems instead of being accountants and detectives.

Playing this unpleasant role is a major reason why so many young college graduates leave the welfare departments.

Mrs. Wilda Mooney, who heads the Garfield District office on the west side of Chicago—which covers an eight-square-block area housing between 9,000 and 10,000 people, roughly a third of them on welfare—is budgeted for 40 caseworkers. She has 29.

"Many of our people are very idealistic when they come to us," she says. "But then they find out they have discouragingly large caseloads; the pressures are high; the paperwork almost overwhelming; and they have very little time to work with people as individuals."

Pay is a problem. In Chicago a young college graduate starts at $550 a month. Other agencies—schools, probation, mental health —are competing for the same workers. The family court starts probation officers at $700 a month.

Many social workers aren't really social workers—they have degrees in music, liberal arts, or some other subject. Most come from middle-class homes and have little idea what it is like to be hungry or to live in teeming squalor. While many are both dedicated and idealistic, others—especially some of the men—are misfits trying to find themselves. Emotionally they may have as many problems as their clients, sometimes more.

And while the best may see a welfare mother once or twice a month—even more often—few have time to work with children. Nor can they do much to solve the problems of the families.

Too little time for 'causalities'

"We go from one emergency to another," says Eugene McKenna, assistant director of child welfare in Greeley, Colo. "There is a strong correlation between ADC families and delinquency. We get the families when their problems begin, but all we do is work with symptoms. There are things we would like to try, but we need smaller caseloads."

In New York City, Commissioner Jack R. Goldberg says essentially the same thing.

"We are really treating only the symptoms," he says. "We have not put enough time into causalities.

"We call the welfare system a 'helping' system, but primarily we dispense money. And that is not really rehabilitative. Money in and of itself isn't enough. And yet we need more money to do the things that really need to be done.

"What we see of institutionalization of kids tells us this isn't the answer. The choice is either to maintain the child and his family or provide a substitute family. We have too long tended to rely on institutions. They cost a great deal and give very little.

"We've got to strengthen what family there is for these youngsters. The answer is to be selective—to discover which children can be helped at home and which ones should go into foster homes.

Department challenged

"That brings up another point. We've got to juice up the pay for foster parents. We've got to get more foster homes. And better foster homes. Some are as ugly as sin."

Mr. Goldberg sees welfare working more closely with schools to prevent delinquency and end the poverty cycle.

"How do you help the poor family get into the mainstream of American life? We've got to do a better job of preparing the kids for the work world. He turns 11 or so, and he begins to see everybody older dropping out of school. Somebody has to pick him up at this point, because this is where these kids start to fall through the crack. Either the school has to pick him up or they have to bring us in."

While foster care is almost always better than cold, overcrowded, brutal institutions, more and more people are challenging the welfare department on their neglect of children placed in these homes. Some girls become unpaid servants; others are mistreated, rejected, and ignored.

Just as youngsters in detention homes and jails are forgotten by caseworkers, so this paper found that those in foster homes may not be seen for months, unless the child runs away or the foster parent complains about the youngster's behavior.

In New York City the welfare department contracts foster-care services with a large number of private agencies—a number of them seriously understaffed. Many of these agencies neglect casework, according to a lengthy memo circulated at a high level in the welfare department but not released to the public.

The memo also points out that the welfare department itself has long negected "providing casework services to children living with parents or relatives in their own homes."

Then it raises other questions that can be asked nationally:

1. Why is one child in foster care when his brothers and sisters are being cared for by their own parents?

2. If removal of one child involved questions of neglect, are there similar problems with respect to the children remaining at

home? Has an evaluation been made currently of the care being received by the children at home?

3. Conversely, if the parents are providing adequate care for children at home, why do one or more children remain in foster care? Is it possible, through giving parents help with financial or other problems, to return the child in care to his own family?

Far more work must be done with the parents when a child is removed from his natural home. The goal is to upgrade the child's home so that he can be returned.

Aid needed for parents

Standards for child-care service developed by the Child Welfare League of America note that "it is essential to recognize the conflicting feelings aroused by [the parent's] inability to fulfill the parental role, by the necessity for placing their child away from his own home, and by the child's and their own relationship with the foster family.

"Appropriate services should be made available to help parents with health, economic, marital, personality, and other problems so that they can resume their parental responsibilities. . . ."

Many, many more good foster homes are needed if children in trouble are to be helped. In New York City, where most children are placed through private agencies, many dependent and neglected children are ignored until their behavior is serious enough to send them to reform school. The memo mentioned earlier reports a shortage of homes for:

● "Negro and Puerto Rican infants who are available for adoption or who do not have functioning families.

● "Children aged 12 and over who need foster care for the first time. Many remain in shelter or in situations of neglect at home. Older teen-agers may be lodged in furnished rooms without adult care or supervision.

● "Children of large family groups. Foster homes are hard to find; several institutions have age limitations or serve boys only or girls only, thus separating brothers and sisters.

● "Physically handicapped children. Those who are blind, deaf, have cerebral palsy, or use crutches are not generally accepted, even though otherwise free of problems.

● "Children with medical problems, such as diabetes or heart disease, who require special supervision or care.

● "Children with serious emotional or psychiatric disorders, especially if diagnosed psychotic, or with history of state-hospital care, or of setting fires.

● "Retarded children who are not defective enough for state school but who need special educational planning and help in learning daily tasks.

● "Children with a combination of the above characteristics or 'problems.' " [The memo might have added all youngsters who have been picked up by police — even for minor charges. This is a problem in nearly every city.]

Reorganization urged

As already noted, a guaranteed annual wage could provide one step toward improving the operation of welfare departments. This should be set high enough, experts say, so that families can live at more than a subsistence level, yet with incentives to encourage them to help themselves.

But beyond the guaranteed wage, welfare leaders see a need to reorganize the entire public-welfare system. They would like to see all helping services under one umbrella: education; mental health; physical health; counseling; family planning; perhaps even probation and parole.

The juvenile court should be used only as a last resort—if at all. As this series has pointed out, few juvenile judges are prepared to resolve complex family problems and too often solve them in hurting, simplistic ways.

Since all children go to school, the reorganized welfare services should be attached to the school. Each service, including education, should be made available to all parents and children alike. It should be made mandatory (through the court) in extreme cases.

Beyond this, existing services should be expanded: Head Start for preschool children; day care for mothers who must work; and homemaker services for the home that is not functioning as it should.

Homemaker service used

Mr. Goldberg, of New York, like so many others, stresses the value of homemaker services as an alternative to taking children from parents.

"It must be broadened and expanded," he says. "Emergency intervention in this way is a significant part of the answer."

In several sections of the country, homemaker services are being used when there is a physical crisis in the home and the mother is ill and cannot clean, cook, and otherwise care for her family.

A booklet issued by the United States Department of Health, Education, and Welfare points out that "losing a parent and being placed in strange surroundings is an unhappy experience for any child. He may become extremely upset or seem apathetic and in a state of shock. Homemaker services allow the child to keep his familiar surroundings rather than experience the hurt of placement during a stressful period in his life."

Not only are these services used when the mother is ill or out of the home, but "in many other situations which upset families: when a new baby arrives; when the mother is absorbed in the care of a member of the family who is seriously ill or handicapped; or when a mother's poor housekeeping skills result in neglect of the children and conflict in her marriage.

"The homemaker is usually a middle-aged, motherly woman, selected for her ability to get along well with others and for her love of children as well as for her housekeeping skills. The agency employing the homemaker gives her some special training, and the child-welfare worker counsels and advises her during the time she is caring for the family. The worker also continues to help the family during the homemaker's stay in the family.

"The length of time a homemaker remains in a family varies with the family's need for her services and agency policies. All variations are found: short-time, long-time, and indefinite arrangements.

Continuity sought

"The homemaker does not supplant the mother but tries, when possible, to carry on the plan of living that the mother has established. Behind the homemaker service is the idea that the family is important in our society.

"The use of a homemaker can often swing the balance in favor of holding the family together during times of crisis."

Some welfare officials suggest that the homemaker service could be the first step in a career ladder for women who are on welfare and want to work. While being trained to help other families, their care of their own families would improve; and when they begin bringing home a paycheck they become productive members of society, rather than a burden to taxpayers.

The cost of housing one youngster in even a mediocre reform school is, in 1969, roughly $8,000 a year. One homemaker paid $5,000 or $6,000 a year can not only care for several children in one family but may be able to serve two or more families in a year.

And in addition to the institutional cost, other figures in the traditional system must be considered: police, probation, court staff, detention, parole—not to mention the damage a child can do that leads him into the court process, or the damage the court and correctional process does to the child.

Thus an effective homemaker could become one of the most economical ways to help children in trouble—especially before serious trouble begins. This service is just one suggestion being made.

Adoptive parents aided

Michio Suzuki, chief of the social-service division of the California Department of Social Welfare, points out that many children who are in foster care have no homes to return to. He notes the value of giving aid to adoptive parents—people who are good, loving foster parents but are financially unable to adopt and care for a child without outside help.

This reporter found hundreds of children without homes locked up in reform schools longing to call someone "Mom and Dad."

John Ballard, executive director of the private Welfare Council of Metropolitan Chicago, sees traditional welfare failing because society has had a "negative, repressive attitude" toward families in trouble.

"What we spend is too little, and it is pouring money down a rathole," he says, "because of the absence of any caring for that child."

Beyond putting helping services under one roof, he would set goals—not unlike the goal of putting a man on the moon established by the Kennedy administration a few years ago:

Instead of scattered shots — the current antipoverty program's approach — careful, thoughtful planning would follow the goal setting. Then the appropriate steps would be taken—methodically doing what is needed to eliminate hunger, to strengthen the family, to eliminate slum housing, to check crime.

Solution sighted

In this newspaper's year-long study of children in trouble it has become convincingly clear that this—along with greater citizen involvement—may be the solution, the panacea so many people are seeking. And the cost would not be prohibitively high.

There is far too much waste in existing programs—uncorrelated projects full of cracks that children slip through, as Mr. Goldberg points out.

Existing programs are top-heavy administratively, bogged down in producing paper, inefficient.

But the framework for change is available: the Department of Health, Education, and Welfare. One solution to much of the paperwork is being considered: the guaranteed annual wage. And effective programs are known: schools like those in

Hughson, Calif.; day care and homemaker services; halfway houses, foster homes, and small, specialized institutions like forest camps; and local volunteer, community involvement.

The Nixon administration has already touched on some of these points. But much more is needed.

The Kennedy administration will be remembered for setting a space goal: men on the moon by 1970. That goal is about to be reached. The present administration has an opportunity to be remembered for setting an even more important goal: doing something meaningful about the problems, of children in trouble.

From the public-welfare notebook . . .

It has long been said that public agencies designed to assist families in trouble fail because they offer fragmented, ineffectual services.

Chicago, long concerned by this, asked Miss Betty Begg, director of correctional services, Department of Human Resources, to document actual case histories from public records.

The following transcript (altered slightly for clarification) covers a 20-year span for a Chicago welfare family from the day it arrived from the South. Its experience is typical. Conflict of names, children who appear but are not accounted for, and other points of confusion are the result of many officials' handling the case without cross-checking data.

1946

Family structure: Edna Smith; son Calvin Jones; father George Jones (deserted in 1938).

Employment: Mother worked Dec. '45 to April, '46, when plant closed. Worked as maid June 1, $83 per month. Factory, Sept. 30, '46; Jan. 8, '49, $34.68 per week.

Income maintenance: Applied for Aid for Dependent Children in April and May. ADC application rejected June 19.

Housing: $14 per month apartment.

1949

Family structure: mother and 3 children by marriage to Jones (2 boys, 1 girl).

Income maintenance: Applied for relief. Eligible for general assistance Jan. 26. Reapplied for relief Nov., referred for ADC, 3 children.

1950

Family structure: mother and 4 children: Harry Black, born Feb. 5. Father's whereabouts unkwn. Nov. 10 Calvin sent to Ala. Mother and 3 children in home. Dec. 5 Calvin returns and daughter Helen sent to California.

Income maintenance: Mar. 10 applied for ADC for 4 children. Granted. July 3, 2 men found in apt. July 11, night visit, 2 men found. July 14, special investig., no men found. Aug. 16, relief stopped until mother explains management. Aug. 21 case closed, lack of info. Oct. 7 caseworker contacted by state senator: children are starving, mother in CCH [Cook County Hospital]. Nov. 27 check withheld until rent receipt is received. Dec. 13 Mrs. S. withdraws application for [daughter?] Helen. However info is so contradictory all money withheld. Dec. 24 case closed, no contact.

Health care: referral for medical care Feb. 5, includ. abortion.

Education: Dec. children don't attend school, no clothes. Dec. 5, school verifies No. 1 & No. 2 sons enrolled.

1951

Employment: domestic & factory work, salary unknown.

Income maintenance: June 31, application for ADC rejected.

Health care: Dec. 28, Mrs. S. pregnant, referred for ADC.

1952

Family structure: Jan. 2 Calvin, 14, in Ala.; Arthur, 12, in Mo., Margaret, 11, back in Chgo. Jan. 29 Oscar Smith born, father's whereabouts unk. Nov. 28 Jack & Helen in Mississippi; Calvin living in Ala.

Income maintenance: Jan. 2 application for aid rejected. Apr & May four applications for ADC; all rejected. June 6 CCDPA [Cook County Department of Public Aid] request ADC for Mrs. Smith. Oct. 1 IPAC [Illinois Public Aid Commission] certificate #97, ADC effective. Oct. 31 inquiry from CCDPA: Why Mrs. S. ineligible compensation? Dec. 18 Mrs. S. continues on ADC.

Health care: Nov. 28 Oscar has ear infection.

1953

Income maintenance: Apr. 13 ADC continues.

1954

Family stucture: Jan. 16 James born; father unknown; Mrs. S. met him once.

Income maintenance: Feb. 5 James added to ADC role. July 30 thru Nov. 22 redetermination of eligibility.

Housing: Moved to another apt., 6 rms., $45 a month.

1955

Employment: Domestic work summer '55, to May, '56, $32 per week (5 days).

Income maintenance: June 8 thru Sept. 28 redetermination of eligibility.

Housing: Summer, '55, to May, '56, 2 boarders pd. $32 per month.

1956

Family structure: April, Calvin marries. Mrs. S. rarely hears from Jack/Helen in South.

Employment: May '56-April '57 domestic work. $50 per week.

Income maintenance: April 11-Apr. 24 redetermination of eligibility. May 18 referral for special Investi. Dept. of Inv. & Frauds. Nov. 19 redetermination of eligibility.

1957

Family structure: Calvin now in Army, has two children.

Employment: May, '56-Apr. '57, domestic work. $50 per wk.

Income maintenance: Apr. 18, grant canceled, fraud suspected. April 25, Mrs. S. applies for assistance for self & 3 children — illness. May, applies for CHA [Chicago Housing Authority] housing. May 21, request for special investig. re Walter Thomas. June 12, request for special investig. re Walter Thomas. ADC canceled. IPAC investigating.

Health care: Apr., Mrs. S. claims asthma; can't work, not under medical care. June 19, Oscar has infected nose — authorization for care. July 18 CCH refers Mrs. S. to Northwestern Clinic for Asthma.

Housing: May 21, new boarder $8 per week.

1958

Income maintenance: Application for general assistance 11/12, Calvin Jones (now out of Army).

1959

Family structure: Children — Harry, Oscar, James; no father in household.

Income maintenance: Case closed; Calvin Jones employed at photo company 2/13. Edna Smith (mother) application for disability assistance 8/30.

Health care: Edna Smith: authorization for medical supplies & services (bronchial asthma).

1960

Income maintenance: redetermination of eligibility 8/30.

1961

Health care: Patient at eye clinic (Oscar).

1962

Family structure: Oscar runs away 6/14.

Income maintenance: redetermination of eligibility 3/5 and 6/14.

Trouble with law: Attempted burglary (Oscar).

Health care: Edna Smith — severe bronchial asthma, Northwestern Univ. Medical School clinics 4/24. Child Guidance Clinic 3 times per week (Oscar).

Education: School reports one child in 5th grade with poor grades; no truancy.

1963

Family structure: Mrs. Smith claims to be having trouble with her boys.

Income maintenance: Continued eligibility for ADC 12/26.

Trouble with law: Runaway (Oscar) 4/20. Runaway (Oscar) and curfew 5/26.

Health care: Mrs. Smith attends allergy clinic at Northwestern Univ. 2/15. Edna Smith dentist 4/24. Edna Smith asthma continues 8/26.

Education: Oscar in elementary school 4/23.

Housing: Mrs. Smith tries to get into public housing project 8/26.

Leisure: Oscar referred Lawson YMCA.

1964

Family structure: Oscar's behavior improves 2/8. Oscar cited as a behavior problem 6/22 and 9/16.

Trouble with law: Runaway & curfew (Oscar) 4/2. Shoplifting & truant (Oscar) 10/2. Theft (Oscar) 10/8.

Education: Mrs. Smith wants Oscar transferred back to school; she is advised to leave him in Montefiore until he is ready to enter high school 9/16.

1965

Family structure: Family (Oscar, Harry, James, Calvin Jones) in Memphis, Tenn., & Mrs. Smith. Harry cited as conduct problem, but Oscar behavior improves 3/5. Mrs. Smith says sons are poorly disciplined 6/3. Mother wants to divest herself from sons' wrongdoings—amoral atmosphere in home. Harry's antisocial behavior will continue as long as he remains at home. Removal advised 7/22.

Clinician notes that crucial factor in Oscar's acting out is absence of a father and lack of supervision by mother 8/30. Mother glad Oscar committed to reform school by IYC [Illinois Youth Commission]. She says their relationship was a good one. She is willing to be primary placement resource when Oscar is returned to the community 8/30. Mother gets subtle gratification out of antisocial behavior of boys, notes probation officer 11/26.

Employment: Part-time Northwestern Univ. 7/22.

Income maintenance: ADC $204 per month 8/30.

Trouble with law: Burglary (James) 1/11. Burglary warrant served (James). Alias summons (James) 2/15. Adjudication finding dismissed (James). Theft of weapon from mother (James) 4/6. Delinquent (Oscar) 5/11. Delinquent burglary (James) 8/10. Failure to appear in court (Oscar) 8/10. Runaway (Oscar) 8/11. Assault (Oscar) 8/12. Habitual runaway (Oscar) recommitted to IYC 8/13. Selling firearms, theft from home (Oscar) 8/16. 1st SB recommended for Oscar 8/30. Transfer order Springfield, Ill., to special education in recep. center Joliet, Ill. (Oscar) 11/7. Runs from DuPage State Boys School. Transfer to 1st SB (Oscar) 11/8.

Health care: Medical history Audy Home exam (Oscar) 5/5. Good health (Oscar) 5/19. Mrs. Smith continues to suffer from asthma 6/8. Good health (Harry) 7/22. Psychological clinical evaluation (Oscar) 8/23. Clinical evaluation (Oscar) 8/30.

Education: Truancy and no academic achievement (Oscar) 5/19. IQ 81, 15 unexcused absences, good classroom habits & attitudes (Oscar) 6/7. Children doing well in school 6/8. Last attended Montefiore school (Oscar) 8/13.

Housing: Moved — apt. on Hudson St.; rent $59.25; sanitary conditions are good 5/19. Cabrini Housing Project, rent $59.00.

Leisure: Attends Sunday School regularly (Oscar) 5/19. Member of St. Dominicks Church, lower North Ctr. (Harry) 7/22.

CHAPTER XII

Efforts to close the police-teen gap

The police cruiser has improved crime-fighting efficiency. But it also has deprived many a neighborhood of its "friendly man on the beat." As such it has become a symbol of today's police-community gap — a gap particularly noticeable among the young. Here is a look at some of the reasons for this gap and at efforts being made to close it.

IT WAS A DARK, WINDY NIGHT IN late October. John Carroll, a plainclothes St. Louis policeman, listened intently to the call on his car radio: "robbery in progress." Quickly he flipped on the siren and the switch that makes his high-beam headlights flash, then pressed down on the accelerator.

The five black teen-agers riding with him grinned as the car moved swiftly through the light traffic. It was the moment they had been waiting for.

Slamming on the brakes when he reached the address mentioned on the police radio, he jumped out of the car. The five youngsters piled out behind him.

Inside, the store owner was being treated for a lump over his eye. Two marked squad cars had arrived minutes before. Already they were gathering information and starting their search of the neighborhood. The youngsters were obviously excited.

St. Louis is just one of the cities trying to change teen-age concepts of the police. John Carroll is a community-relations officer. In the past seven years he has given hundreds of youngsters an opportunity to tour the police headquarters, ask questions, then ride for a night in an unmarked police car.

Police car a barrier?

Yet ironically, the police car itself may be a symbol of the gap between youngsters and the police: The officer who spends his time behind the steel walls of a squad car loses econtact with the neighborhood.

As noted earlier in this series, children from poor homes have trouble relating positively to people who are coolly professional —whether they be store clerks, teachers, or mobile policemen.

Thus the cool professional who skids up to the curb, siren wailing, lights flashing, is not as effective as the officer who is known by name in the neighborhood. In fact, studies indicate that riots have been triggered by a patrolman—unfamiliar with the neighborhood and its people—when he resorts to force.

For a decade or more, respect for the police has been plummeting. Many people blame the Supreme Court and permissive parents. Yet this reporter's studies indicate the real difficulty lies with inadequate police departments and with society at large.

Near-Neanderthal methods—hitting people with clubs to control or restrain them—in the face of civil-rights demonstrators, ghetto unrest, and campus disorders often reinforce the notion that violence carries society's approval.

Violence given approval

And, if polls taken after last year's Democratic National Convention are accurate, that approval is present: A large majority of citizens supported the violent tactics police used to quell the Chicago demonstrations.

While not condoning brutality, police officials often complain that they are unable to hire men of the caliber that once staffed police departments. This reporter's investigations bear this out.

While I met dedicated, socially aware officers, I also found a surprising number of policemen who said they joined the department at least in part because they like guns. Many wear gun tie clips.

Too many policemen, it would appear, are hired not because they know how to deal effectively with people, but because they were (or would make) good marines.

The "friendly man on the beat" is now on wheels

I also found racial prejudice runs high among policemen. In addition, many seem unable to accept change—for instance in dress and hair styles of youth.

Many policemen enjoy a high-speed chase. (Some even seem to enjoy the shoot-out.) One who visits police stations at shift-change time may find an officer who has chased a teen-ager at speeds approaching 90 or 100 miles bragging about it. His fellow officers elevate him almost to hero status —even if someone was seriously injured or killed.

I also found that a large number of youngsters—especially the more immature teen-agers—enjoy playing "cops and robbers" as much as some policemen do.

Vern, a small, 19-year-old Connecticut youth, was serving time for car theft and burglary in the Connecticut Reformatory in Cheshire. His response was typical.

"It isn't I hate cops," he said. "I like the chase. I always knew I'd get caught sooner or later. When the cops are after me with their sirens and stuff, I feel good. I don't know why."

'Standin' on the corner'

I found the greatest hostility toward police among the highly visible minority groups— not only black, Puerto Rican, and Mexican-Americans, but also white teen-agers with long hair and strange costumes.

Many of them had been stopped and searched by police for what the youngsters called no reason—'we were just standin' on the corner.' This is a common complaint in slum neighborhoods, and it can be verified both by minority-group adults and by policemen themselves.

Police must recognize that they have an added responsibility when dealing with children in trouble. When such youngsters come in contact with police, they are far more likely to go to reform school than those who are handled by other agencies — mental health for example. This even when offenses are identical.

Why? Because, except in cities where the probation staff does the screening, the police decide who goes to court and who does not. Thus the police play a judgelike role.

Even for youngsters who would not be classed as "in trouble," the first contact with a policeman may be negative: a traffic violation.

Attitudes studied

The most meaningful study on teen-age attitudes toward police was made at the University of Cincinnati by Dr. Robert G. Portune, head of the department of secondary education.

Dr. Portune and his team of researchers started in by measuring attitudes toward police of youngsters between the ages of 12 and 16. They found that not only were young people "ignorant of the nature of law and the mission and function of law enforcement" but that "police officers who have initial contacts with these youngsters were ignorant of the nature of early adolescence."

Among the study's other findings:

• When youngsters enter the 7th grade, their attitudes toward the law and police are significantly more favorable than when they finish 9th grade.

• Attitudes vary by socio-economic level. The lower the level the poorer the attitude.

• Attitudes vary by sex. The attitude of girls is significantly more favorable than that of boys.

• Attitudes vary by race. White attitudes toward police are considerably better than Negro.

• Attitudes vary by ability groups in school. The poor students have more unfavorable attitudes.

• Boys who go to church regularly have attitudes more favorable than those who do not. Girls who attend church seem to have the same attitudes as those who do not.

• It takes approximately two years for a significant change in attitudes to occur, and when this does occur it is in an unfavorable direction.

• The school curriculum has nothing built in to change attitudes in the direction of respect for law and law enforcement.

• Police training curriculum has nothing specifically designed to change attitudes or to inform the officer as to the nature of the early adolescent.

Conference then called

The researchers' next step was to design educational programs both for police officers and for junior high schools. A conference was called in 1966. Juvenile police officers and junior high school administrators from 15 states attended. Soon appropriate material was produced.

For the youngsters, emphasis is on the student discovering the need for rules, laws, and law enforcement on his own. A classroom of eighth graders, for example, is given balls of various color, sizes, and shapes. The teacher prepares a place for scoring on the blackboard. Then she writes down the word "start." But there are no rules.

First the youngsters stand around staring at each other. Then chaos develops, says Dr. Portune.

"Within about three minutes the youngsters are ready to sit down and discuss what is wrong with the game, and why there can be no winner. From this they begin to see the necessity for rules—fair rules."

In April, 1967, the curriculum was placed in 7th, 8th, and 9th-grade classes in 12 greater Cincinnati schools. A good cross section of both suburban and inner-city, hard-core children took part.

'World of rules' dealt with

Incorporated as a six-weeks' course in standard social-studies classes, the 7th-graders now study the "World of Rules" — from the laws of gravity and motion to rules in the home, the school, and the community. One assignment involves studying school rules and then changing a rule by approaching those who make and enforce them— whether student council or administration.

In the 8th grade the subject is called the "World of Games," and not only includes discovering the need for rules to play games or in organized sporting events, but the need for someone to officiate. This eventually includes "The Game of Life in the Community."

The 9th-grade unit is called the "World of Laws" and involves discovering the necessity for laws. Among other things, students plan a school SAP assembly. SAP stands for "subtract a policeman." Emphasis is on making sure youths don't do things that subtract a policeman from his normal duties in the community.

All children were tested to discover their attitudes about law and law enforcement. Then they were divided into the group taking the six-week courses and a control group that received no special curriculum.

Eight weeks later all students were re-tested. The experimental classes, in every instance, significantly changed toward a more favorable view of law and law enforcement. Those in the control groups did not change their views or grew more hostile toward the police and the law.

Not only could this be shown statistically, but a student-by-student analysis showed every child in the experimental classes had an improved attitude toward police and the law.

Because of the success of the program in Cincinnati-area schools, a conference for police-training officers and school-curriculum directors was held on the campus in the summer of 1967.

Then more federal funding was made available, and the project was tried in Rochester, N.Y., Tampa, Fla., and Fort Smith, Ark. Now some 6,000 students have been involved, always with the same results. The grant runs out the end of this month — but already several hundred schools have asked for material.

In recent years leading police officials have been trying to bring about change in their field. But too many have not understood the problems.

Better screening needed

Men like Chicago's Orlando W. Wilson (now retired) saw the answer in highly sophisticated equipment, computers, more squad cars responding faster, better weapons, and greater professionalism. Professionalism is still often considered the "new" approach in the police field, and too few of the 40,000 independent police departments scattered across the United States have training programs beyond a few hours on the pistol range.

What is clearly needed is more careful screening, and then training that will make policemen more effective human beings.

This is stressed by Dr. John D. Gerletti, director of the Delinquency Control Institute at the University of Southern California. He suggests that training for interpersonal relationships is far more important than learning how to shoot straight.

"We tend to look at law enforcement in terms of control, rather than prevention," he says. "But the solution is not through supression. Education and [delinquency] prevention has to be the answer. And I think the average policeman is quite capable of handling this wider role."

The highly effective Delinquency Control Institute was developed 23 years ago. Each year 50 to 60 police juvenile officers have taken part in a 12-week program on the campus. Next year it will be expanded to 100 policemen.

Yet this program and a few others scattered across the country scarcely make a dent: It is estimated that there are more than 400,000 policemen in the United States — many of whom come in contact with juveniles.

Program expanding

Dr. Gerletti reports another problem: "We pull a man out of a police department and in 12 weeks we get him turned on. Then we send him back. Unfortunately, the community and the police chief too often don't know how to use him."

Now the institute is working with police chiefs and with communities, hoping to turn them on, too.

In the fall 12 officers from Ventura County—from local police departments, the state, and the sheriff's office—will study as a team three days a week and do research in the county two days a week. If this is effective, similar programs will be tried in a Midwestern state and an Eastern city.

Each summer a seminar is held at the

University of Minnesota for those dealing with youngsters in trouble — including policemen. Richard Clendenen, professor of criminal law administration, who heads the program, places great emphasis on helping officers understand human behavior — both their own and that of others, especially youngsters from minority groups.

While those who attend return home with helpful insights, too few of the nation's police are involved.

More cities have opened police academies in recent years. Existing recruit training programs have been improved. And in-service training programs are being beefed up.

A delicate mission

In New York City officers now receive some 65 hours of instruction in delinquency and the causes of delinquency, says Lt. Michael J. McNulty of the advanced and specialized training section.

The program is designed to teach officers that:

● They often represent the first agency to identify and confront delinquent youngsters;

● This confrontation plays a vital role in shaping the youngsters views toward the law, police, and courts;

● Police contact with errant youngsters frequently occurs at an age before the commitment to delinquency is strong, and thus proper intervention can help these children;

● For this reason officers must be alert to the needs and problems of the youngsters;

● It is imperative that policemen focus their attention on negative forces in the social environment and ferret out corruption and criminal influences that threaten the healthy development of young people;

● Prevention of delinquency is the goal of police-youth programs.

Chicago's police department, like many others, is working to develop an effective community-relations program, encouraging those who live in a neighborhood to help grapple with delinquency. An "Officer Friendly" visits elementary schools.

'Welfare Wagon' joined

In South Pasadena, Calif., and in other cities policemen often accompany the Welcome Wagon hostess to help greet newcomers. They briefly discuss local laws, ask to shake the hands of the children in the family.

Flint, Mich., pioneered the use of police officers in schools—not to maintain order, but to serve as counselors. Other cities have modified this program. In some schools, policemen teach classes.

This, and other programs springing up, raise important questions about the role of the policeman in society. More and more he is being asked to function as a social worker. It is clear, then, that he must be better trained. Further, there must be greater co-ordination between police departments and other agencies involved with juveniles—the welfare departments, mental-health departments, public schools, and juvenile courts.

Obviously the policeman cannot, by himself, solve all of society's pressing problems — slums, family breakdown, hunger, alcoholism, poor correctional institutions. But he can become more effective as a human being. This is why police-sponsored Boy Scout troops, boys clubs, Little League teams, and other such organizations are beneficial.

One of the most interesting experiments along this line can be found in New York City. "Police-Youth Dialogue" sends 10 policemen and 30 youngsters to a camp each weekend (a different precinct goes each week.)

Leadership looked for

The project manager, Sgt. Alfred Toefield, explains that the youngsters are picked because they are leaders or potential leaders. They are often those an officer is having trouble with on his beat.

The camp is located on the grounds of Fort Cotten in Whitestone, Queens. Each Saturday morning policemen who have volunteered to take part drop by to pick up the youngsters. The youngsters (also volunteers) have parental consent to go. All ride together to camp by bus.

Stolen bicycles that have not been claimed are used around the camp. Youngsters fish for flounder and eel from a pier; go into neighboring parks; visit a historical monument being built; play baseball—all with the police officers. In civilian clothing, the officers function as big brothers or counselors.

Then in the evening the group gathers around for a healthy give-and-take discussion.

Youngsters ask policemen why some beat children; why other officers are crooked; why some have double standards; or why they have to play the tough role.

In turn, the policemen challenge the young men on their behavior—shouting taunts from a half block away, sniffing glue or using drugs, fighting police.

It is this kind of open dialogue that holds the most promise. Every police department in the nation could profit from such a program.

'Plenty of recreation' — one key to helping children in trouble

CHAPTER XIII

Your community <u>can</u> do something

During a year's study of children in trouble this newspaper
has found many communities are apathetic toward
the plight of these children. A search for an "ideal"
community turned up four in Michigan that, in composite,
could well serve as a model for the rest of the nation.
The key: local concern for strengthening the family and
providing constructive alternatives to reform school.

N O COMMUNITY IN AMERICA IS DO-
ing enough for children in trouble. Too
many, in fact, damage children and raise
the crime rate through apathy, ignorance,
and neglect.

This became obvious as this newspaper
searched the United States for two counties
—one urban, one rural—to serve as models
for the rest of the nation.

One community had an outstanding judge
and strong probation department, another
a constructive welfare system; still a third
had widespread community concern and
volunteer involvement. But all lacked the
across-the-board excellence and determination to solve the problems that produce
delinquency.

This newspaper's search for the ideal
county was based on four premises: (1) The
local community has a responsibility to
children in trouble; (2) crime prevention is
better and far cheaper than crime fighting;
(3) the answer lies in strengthening both
the child and the family, not in hurting children or tearing the family apart; and (4)
the efforts of a single institution (the school,
the police, or the court, for example) are
not sufficient to resolve the problem.

Criteria established

This reporter looked for a community
that had:
● Not only strong schools with few dropouts and creative programs for "hand"
children, but a system that turned their
schools into year-round, seven-day-a-week,
family-oriented community centers.
● An uplifting welfare department rather
than one that perpetuates poverty.
● A full range of private or public
agencies providing family services: marriage counseling; mental-health clinics;

dental and physical health services, including services for the indigent; job training
and placement for the unemployed and
underemployed; homemakers to help disabled mothers; legal aid; financial counseling; a consumer-protection group; and
a system to coordinate these services and
eliminate red tape.
● A program that was well on the way to
eradicating slum housing through aggressive building-code enforcement and in other
ways.

Participation stressed

● A qualified juvenile judge; adequate
and creative probation staff; and a variety
of alternatives for children who cannot be
helped at home.
● Proper detention facilities — plus shelter care for children in trouble but not involved in delinquent acts.
● Group homes and foster homes for all
children unable to remain in their own
homes.
● Strong churches that reached out to
the community and daily proved their usefulness.
● Active citizen participation in a variety
of volunteer programs.
● Year-round recreation programs —
with something for children who are not
well coordinated, who lack athletic skills,
or those who have other interests; neighborhood parks and playgrounds; and a camping program for children of the poor.
● A well-trained police department that
emphasized crime prevention and community relations rather than billy-club
toughness.

While no single urban area measured up

There are alternatives to reform school

on all counts, four in Michigan—if combined —would come close to the ideal:

Flint for its school program; Oakland County for its outstanding citizen-participation program, county institutions, and court and probation department; Grand Rapids for its court, probation, detention, shelter care, and foster homes; and Kalamazoo for its school and work program for dropouts.

Program described

The Flint school program is exciting. While the typical school is used 1,400 hours a year, the 52 schools in Flint average 3,800. Each school has a full-time, trained community-activities coordinator to see that schools are utilized continually.

Evenings and Saturdays one finds families swimming, Scout troops meeting, community groups holding discussions about local problems, families roller-skating in the gym, and people going to school.

While about 2,000 youngsters graduated from high schools in Flint this year, roughly 1,000 adults also received diplomas.

Another 80,000 adults [out of a population of only a little over 200,000] were enrolled in 1,200 adult-education classes. Subjects ranged the gamut—how to stretch your food dollar, child growth and development, shorthand, typing, sewing, welding, landscaping, jobs (where and how to get them), drawing and painting, music, cake decorating, how to start a small business, electronics, and beagle breeding.

Counseling utilized

A plainclothes policeman works in every school. When a child gets in trouble in the neighborhood that his school serves, the officer takes the case and acts as a counselor far more often than he takes the child to court.

A personalized curriculum program has been developed for dropouts and those about to drop out.

These students get special counselors who work out a school schedule that better fits their needs. For many of these students, the counselor finds a job either in the mornings or afternoons, and some get school credit for their work.

During the summer, some 800 boys go to camp. While most have indigent parents, others have prosperous parents who don't seem to care about their children. Another 200 take part in two-week work programs on area farms in a program supported by the Neighborhood Youth Corps. This spring alone another 10,000 children made one-day farm visits.

Some 600 fifth and sixth graders are members of a police cadet program — community-service activities in which policemen serve as group leaders.

Community service noted

In a new program, 20 boys and 20 girls, most of them black and all juniors and seniors in high school, work in their neighborhoods as uniformed community-service officers, providing citizens with information about how to deal with personal or community problems. Paid with Neighborhood Youth Corps funds, many will eventually work for the police department.

A hot-breakfast and hot-lunch program has been provided in selected schools for a decade — but only if the child's mother agrees to come in one week each term to help prepare the meals. The greatest value in this is the training the mother receives in both cooking and nutrition.

(The federal government has expanded this program to 16 schools, but unfortunately the training program is not included in the federally sponsored meals.)

When a child comes to school dirty or otherwise uncared for or when other problems develop in the home, one of 18 community school counselors takes over.

These are unusual women — many of them Negro — who may put the children's clothing through the school washing machine, teach mothers how to use their small welfare checks more wisely, and see that they get the services they need.

Not long ago one of these counselors, Mrs. Mary Towner, who works on Flint's North Side, found two children new to her school frequently absent. At 9:30 one morning she knocked on the door of their apartment.

Help sought

She was invited in. The room was dark. In one corner she found the mother curled up on a blanket. Across the room the woman's teen-age daughter was on another blanket on the floor with her small illegitimate baby. The two children who should have been in school were running around half naked. There was no furniture and no refrigerator. The cooking was done in an old electric frying pan. The woman had been on leave from work because of illness for nearly a year and now had no money at all.

Mrs. Towner went to the welfare department, health department, and Salvation Army for immediate aid. Then with the help of a county extension worker she taught the mother how to spend her food money more wisely, how to bake, and to make nutritious, low-cost meals.

She tried to help the mother with a drinking problem and saw that the children received much-needed dental care. Then one day, after she found four men in the apartment, Mrs. Towner began working to improve the woman's feeling of self-worth so that she would not let herself be used by men.

The case is typical.

The Flint program, backed by the Charles Stewart Mott Foundation, has not ended delinquency. But Dr. Peter Clancy, the associate superintendent of schools in charge of Mott projects, believes that in the last five years a "dent has been made" in delinquency rates. Those rates are, in fact, declining.

A few miles southeast of Flint is Oakland County, a cluster of communities with a combined population of roughly a million. This county is a wealthy "bedroom" area for Detroit. Yet it also includes Pontiac, a middle-class community of about 90,000, as its county seat, and such low-income areas as heavily black Royal Oak Township.

Committees formed

In few areas in the United States is there such citizen involvement in delinquency prevention. Now 27 communities have formed court supportive youth-assistance committees.

These committees are made up of housewives, ministers, businessmen, and representatives from public and private welfare agencies, Boy and Girl Scouts, YMCAs, school boards, police departments, local recreation departments, a child-guidance clinic, and other groups and agencies.

Each group is sponsored by the court, the school board, and municipal government. Sixteen paid caseworkers spend at least one day each week working with (and for) the 27 committees.

The committees have one goal: delinquency prevention.

This means both working on the community level — creating recreational opportunities, holding family-improvement seminars, and offering other group services — and tackling problems of children and families on an individual basis.

Many children who break the law for the first time do not even go to court. Instead, they are referred to the committees. Once the referral is made, the child cannot be taken to court for that offense.

When a referral is made, the child's family is told that the program is voluntary. The family can reject the help, but few do.

"Word gets around that this is a good group. A group that really wants to work. In Southfield, people come to us with almost every problem you can imagine," says Leon Avedisian, a businessman and president of the Youth Assistance Advisory Council.

Room divided

When a child is referred and special help is needed, a subcommittee of the youth-assistance committee does a case study. These are trained professionals: a school counselor, a psychologist, psychiatrist, social worker, physician, and representative from the child-guidance clinic. They develop a treatment plan, then appropriate agencies are called in.

If the child needs a job for spending money, if the home is overcrowded, or if a similar problem exists, members of the youth assistance committee may step in. In Birmingham, Mich., not long ago eight children were sleeping in one room. So members of the committee brought in hammers and saws and constructed some temporary partitions until a better solution could be found.

Usually the entire family receives services. For, as this series has pointed out, most children in trouble come from families in trouble.

Although the support for the program is widespread, there is still some concern voiced—particularly among police—about the program's effectiveness in dealing with hard-core delinquents. Lt. David Putnam, of the Waterford Township Police Department complains:

"We fall over backward trying to keep a kid from getting a juvenile record. But we get so weary picking up a kid day after day after day. Youth Assistance Committees need more staff to do a really effective job."

When it is necessary for a child to go to court, the county has provided Children's Village (a detention and shelter-care complex in Pontiac) and Camp Oakland (which involves several programs).

Children's Village, which opened in 1965, is located on a 57-acre tract not far from the new courthouse on the edge of Pontiac. There are three brick, ranch-style units: one for emotionally disturbed children, many awaiting admission to a state mental hospital; another for neglected boys 9 to 16 years old; and a third for delinquent boys 14 to 16.

Replacement sought

There are two older units closer to the courthouse: an overcrowded two-story detention center constructed in 1928 and a shelter home for dependent and neglected children opened in the early 1950's.

Except for the detention center—which officials hope to replace soon—each unit is small. A new unit for girls is desperately needed. Many whom it is not necessary to lock in must, at present, be housed in the detention center.

Almost all children attend school daily. The day I was there many children went on evening field trips. Bowling, swimming, hiking, roller-skating, and other activities are a regular part of the program.

Camp Oakland is located on an old estate farm in a rural area north of Pontiac. There are two group homes for dependent, neglected, and even delinquent youngsters — Boys Ranch for 20 children, and Girls Ranch, which houses 18 youngsters. Many stay here for two years or longer.

Assignments listed

Children go by bus to school in town. Not only do they have the kind of support and much of the freedom most children have in their own homes, but they bring friends from the community in for parties, overnights, swimming, and hiking. They date children from the public school in town and take part in a full range of school activities.

On the far side of the small lake owned by the camp is the work-education program. The school portion is headed by Gordon Keller, who uses a great deal of programmed instruction, individualized help, and the warm and intimate teaching methods discussed earlier in this series. He is able to help many boys advance two years in a few months.

All the boys have work assignments: landscaping, mowing, road grading with a tractor, and construction projects on the grounds — assisting professional builders.

Beyond this, 500 to 600 youngsters — all of them deprived children from the county — spend two weeks camping. This facility is located on another corner of the lake.

Perhaps most significant is the family camping program. Welfare and other underprivileged mothers bring their children for two weeks—but take part in separate programs.

While the children play and learn under the guidance of carefully selected counselors, the mothers are taught about child care and behavior, take part in group discussions, and find themselves free of nagging concern for a few days.

The camp complex is run by William Matus — the enthusiastic "father" to these children.

In some communities youth-assistance committees send children with special needs on to other summer camps, reports Mrs. Harvey Dise, president of the Birmingham group.

Cooperation a factor

Oakland County's program is noteworthy because it provides a variety of alternatives to reform school. And it is the result of cooperation between an understanding county board of supervisors and compassionate, concerned citizens.

Oakland County did not wait for the state or the federal government to provide funds. It proved the free-enterprise system can care about people.

A major difference between Oakland County and other counties—many with similar percentages of wealthy and middle-class families—is leadership. Oakland County has Circuit Judge Arthur E. Moore, who more clearly understands his leadership role than perhaps any other judge in America.

He has long been supported by the strong professional voice of James Hunt, director of children's services; by a leading businessman, the late Walter Gehrke, president of Detroit's First Federal Savings; and by a host of others.

Leadership is also the key in Grand Rapids, where the detention-home program is much stronger than most in the nation. It includes a good school program, plenty of recreation, and an adequate staff.

The greatest drawback is that it is actually a long-stay institution. It is used in this way because the State of Michigan has been extremely negligent in providing facilities for children. The type of facilities found in Oakland County have just not been built in Grand Rapids.

However, three private agencies — one Protestant, one Roman Catholic, and one nondenominational—handle most dependent and neglected children.

An hour's drive to the south in Kalamazoo is an exciting program called Youth Opportunities Unlimited (YOU).

In what was once a bowling alley I found 30 youngsters packing nuts, bolts, and washers; sorting and packing printed packages; and assembling small highway barricades and the flashing lights that are attached to the barricades.

Similar work was being done in a portable classroom on the detention center grounds.

Although an extremely conservative Republican community, Grand Rapids has, since the 1940's, had an active group of citizens serving as a court advisory council. Among other things, they were able to bring enough pressure on the community to get rid of a wretched detention building a decade ago.

In addition to the detention home, a new shelter for dependent and neglected children has been built. An excellent facility, it is run by the welfare department, which up to now has—in most Michigan counties—been extremely slow in providing needed service for children.

John P. Steketee of Grand Rapids, recently elected juvenile court judge, and Roger L. Lewis, director of court services, are providing the imaginative leadership needed.

Probation officers receive excellent in-service training. Not only have experts been brought into conduct seminars, but Mr. Lewis has been asked to talk to probation officers across the state.

Instead of following the traditional approach, which so often is ineffective, Grand Rapids juvenile probation officers sit down and hammer out a "contract" that bridges conflicts between parent and child.

Since many children in trouble have problem parents, a father may be asked to agree to such a basic need as saying "good morning" to his son each day. Or a mother may agree to get up and cook breakfast for her children each morning in return for good, respectful behavior.

The child also agrees to take other steps to correct his behavior. Emphasis is on getting the child to behave, rather than on how bad he is.

Detention children who are in for long periods — often awaiting placement — can earn weekend passes, bowling trips, and other outside activities.

Parents assessed cost

Volunteers are being used more than in the past, although those from the community have been teaching remedial reading for five years. (The program has sagged since the woman heading it moved.) The Junior League has offered to provide more services.

Youngsters held a car wash during spring vacation and used the money they earned for horseback riding.

Two representatives from the Old Kent Bank recently came in to analyze statistics in the juvenile-court process. Suggested improvements were quickly made.

Sometimes when parents refuse to take their children home (roughly half the children in court last year were runaways or had school or home behavior problems) the court may keep the youngsters in detention and charge the parents for their keep until the parents recognize their responsibility.

In the past year the court worked with the public school system to develop a program for dropouts, using two probation officers and a teacher as instructors. Now some 25 local teachers have volunteered to give up part of their summer vacation to help teach children in trouble.

Work is contracted through local industries. Youngsters — all of them dropouts or near dropouts — are paid on a piecework basis at industrial rates. Those who play or are daydreaming have smaller checks at the end of the week. Thus they are taught that the most industrious and skilled earn the most.

The program is coupled with half-day educational sessions and a job-placement program. While some youngsters return to school, others, after they learn to work, are channeled into industry.

Headed by Ronald Williams, the program began in 1961 with contributions from a Kalamazoo woman. It is run by the Kalamazoo Intermediate School District.

While none of the Michigan community programs are yet adequate to meet the needs of all children in trouble, these communities outdistance most cities in America, providing services that state agencies have failed to provide.

But Michigan has even more going for it: Children's Charter. The organization is dedicated to provide the services needed by the juvenile courts through dialogue and education on the local level.

Children's Charter of the Courts of Michigan (its full title) is largely backed by the W. K. Kellogg Foundation. Over 10 years the foundation has contributed $732,000.

Conferences called

Children's Charter holds conferences for the police, prosecutors, school officials, and court personnel — to help them understand both children in trouble and the role each agency plays. Children's Charter conducts surveys and serves as consultant to individual courts and state-governmental groups.

It also provides small scholarships to large numbers of juvenile-court workers who want to take college courses related to their field.

Children's Charter is run by two men: a former judge, Donald T. Anderson, and a former high-school principal, Eugene S. Thomas.

For a while it appeared that Children's Charter would fade away as the Kellogg grant ran out. Now it appears certain the program will be picked up by Western Michigan University in Kalamazoo.

It is clear from this newspaper's study that the efforts of these Michigan communities in behalf of their children are in the right direction.

CHAPTER XIV

An alternative to detention: attention

If a county's officials provide leadership and if its individual citizens care, children headed for delinquency can be "turned around." This chapter takes a look at two such counties: Scotts Bluff in Nebraska and Boulder in Colorado. Both offer programs that show great promise for helping children in trouble.

MARIAN WAS 12 WHEN SHE WAS ARrested for forging checks and passing them at a clothing store.

A small, plain girl with long black hair, she would have been a prime candidate for reform school in many communities. But not in Scottsbluff, Neb. For in Scottsbluff people care about children in trouble.

Marian is 14 now. For the past two years she has been living as a foster child on a 13,000-acre ranch on the Wyoming border. She has her own horse, is active in 4-H, and is strong, suntanned, and happy.

Marian was born of an incestuous relationship between her father and her older sister, who was twice committed to a mental hospital. When Marian was six, she saw another older sister, who had been caring for her, shot to death by the sister's husband.

Until she was arrested for buying clothes with the forged checks her life had been confused, even desperate.

A good place to be arrested

Marian's case — and dozens of others— show that being arrested in Scotts Bluff County can be the best thing that ever happened to some youngsters.

Much of the credit must go to the county's highly effective juvenile probation officer, James L. Miller, a former policeman and narcotics expert.

Mr. Miller is compassionate, yet firm. He can deal effectively with children in trouble because he has been there. His father and mother were divorced. He describes his childhood home as "tough, with a lot of drinking." Things got so bad that he was placed in a series of foster homes.

From this background he made it through two years of junior college.

Unlike many probation officers with police background, he understands that sending children to reform school can do more harm than good. Thus institutionalization is limited to extreme cases.

At present he has found more than 50 foster homes. They are scattered across western Nebraska. And while some foster parents are given a small amount to care for children, either through the Nebraska Children's Home, or through the Welfare Department, many provide foster care free.

This is the case with Marian's foster parents, who have 14 children of their own. In fact, when Marian's father passed on some months ago and she began receiving $53 a month social security, her foster parents decided they would bank $50 for Marian's higher education, giving her the $3 a month to spend.

When I visited Scottsbluff a few days ago, I found that not only did Marian's foster parents have her and two other foster children, but that they had agreed to accept four more—all from the same family.

Scotts Bluff County is an unusual model for the rest of the nation because it is small, rural, isolated, with limited financial resources, and has serious problems.

Denver nearest city

A large number of poverty-stricken Mexican-Americans live in rundown shacks on Scottsbluff's fringes. And teen-age drug use has been growing through out-of-town students who attend Hiram Scott College — a new four-year institution. (Marijuana grows wild along the roadsides and creek beds.)

Boulder County builds its Attention Homes on trust

Slightly more than 39,000 people make up this high, dry county that is split diagonally by the North Platte River. Half of those live in the adjoining towns of Scottsbluff and Gering.

Located just east of the Wyoming line, about midway between the South Dakota and Colorado borders, the nearest major center is Denver, some 200 miles to the south (and slightly west). Cheyenne, 100 miles southwest, is the nearest medium-sized community.

Cattle ranching and irrigated row crops are the major source of income, with sugar-beet processing the main activity.

Until about four years ago Scotts Bluff handled its juvenile problems in a rather traditional way. County Judge Richard S. Wiles did what he could with limited resources, but far too many children were locked in the awful children's section of the county jail or shipped off to reform school.

Judge Wiles then formed a juvenile-court advisory committee, made up of local citizens. A year later he hired Mr. Miller as his probation officer.

Community 'turned on'

For more than two years the advisory committee struggled along. Then a new minister in town, the Rev. James F. Landrum, was persuaded to take the presidency. The Rev. Mr. Landrum had once taught Sunday school in an Indiana reform school and had helped form two private institutions (Illini Children's Christian Home, St. Joseph; and Indiana Children's Christian Home, Ladoga) for youngsters. Imaginative, determined, he began to devote most of his time to Scotts Bluff County children in trouble.

This was what Judge Wiles and Jim Miller needed. With the strong support of the local radio station, KOLT, and the newspaper, the Star-Herald, Scotts Bluff County "turned on."

Not only did the number of foster homes grow from a handful to more than 50—housing some 65 children in trouble—but other things began to happen.

When I visited Scotts Bluff County, I found 17 committees at work, trying to eliminate juvenile delinquency in various ways.

A summer recreational program had begun that day with a $2,300 grant from the Scottsbluff city fathers and the help of student volunteers. Mayor C. A. Thomas says that next year $7,000 will be available; that $12,000 is being budgeted for the following year; and that eventually his community will have a "full-time, year-round recreational program."

The city became interested in spending money on recreation last fall when Mrs.

Jeannie Westervelt, a former schoolteacher and member of the court advisory committee, began making speeches to service clubs and other groups on the subject.

Fenced playgrounds unlocked

School playgrounds are fenced and had been locked to prevent vandalism. The school board agreed to open them. The city money was used, in part, to hire a recreation director and two assistants for two months. Local groups have donated supplies for arts and crafts. The schools are proving balls and play equipment. And youngsters will be able to rent other games from a mobile recreational unit.

In the basement of the county jail one room is filled with children's clothing donated by local citizens. This was the result of court officials' discovering that many children skipped school, stole, or otherwise got into trouble because they had no shoes or underwear or were poorly dressed.

Jim Miller and others from time to time dipped into their own pockets to provide basic needs for these youngsters.

Parent counseling is used with families of children in trouble. One 17-year-old girl dating college students was constantly in trouble with her mother who (falsely) accused her of using narcotics and being a prostitute. (Her older sister is a prostitute.) Her father was working two jobs and never had time for his family.

How committees cooperate

It was discovered that the girl felt totally rejected. She recalled only one good time in her life—a family camping trip. The mother agreed to take her daughter for two weeks in the Black Hills. The father visited them there. The family got to know each other better, and the girl is not only getting along better, but says she will return to school in the fall.

Sometimes committees work together. One 12-year-old boy arrived in court without underwear and was dressed in rags. He had been picked up as a truant. Mr. Miller took him home, found the family without heat or food, with only a small camping stove to cook on, and the electricity cut off.

The father had disappeared, leaving the mother and five children. She worked as a part-time waitress and as a maid in a cheap hotel to provide food. Welfare turned the family down because they had not lived in the state long enough. When Mr. Miller reached the home, he found the youngsters hadn't eaten for a day and a half.

Clothing was provided. Mr. Miller and others on the council started asking for donations. The newspaper told of the family's need. Soon they had furniture. A job was found for the young mother as a receptionist for a local dentist. The welfare department was persuaded to find her a baby-sitter so the children wouldn't be left alone. The boy went back to school.

Scotts Bluff County also has what it calls the "Listening Post." This, too, is a significant delinquency-prevention program, although not yet fully utilized by the community. Professional counselors make up the committee.

Parents, even children call

Sometimes a parent will call, asking what to do to keep a child from running with the wrong group or one on the edge of delinquency from getting into worse trouble. Now and then children ask for help.

One 17-year-old was picked up by police in a street brawl. (Later it was found he was fighting in self-defense.) His father, an ex-convict, was determined to give the boy a beating, according to Mr. Miller. As usual, the mother opposed this (part of a long-time family battle). The boy, tired of the conflict, and "brighter than either of his parents," called the Listening Post.

The boy had been failing in school. But after a series of family-counseling sessions he is "doing fine." The father now holds a steady job, and the home is relatively calm for the first time in years, according to Mr. Miller.

When counseling fails, the Listening Post has other committees to turn to. A 14-year-old girl was promiscuous and defied her mother. She was first placed on probation, eventually put in a foster home. The mother had wanted the girl "locked up."

The juvenile court advisory committee also has a committee working with school dropouts and tutoring students in reading and other subjects. Students from the Platte Valley Bible College do much of the tutoring.

These students haven't been afraid to tackle the dirty jobs. One Mexican family lived in a rundown shack on the riverbank on a farm owned by an extremely wealthy farmer. The mother passed on. The father supporting his family of 15 by working for the farmer from dawn until after dark at $40 a week.

Mr. Miller learned of the family when one of the children, a 12-year-old boy, was arrested for breaking into a church. He found the children covered with lice, and suffering from malnutrition and a variety of skin diseases. Eight of the children slept in one bed, the father and two boys slept in a second bed, and the rest of the children slept on the floor—pine boards with spaces between them. Their used clothing was burned for heat when it became too filthy to wear. They cooked on a wood fire in a broken-down gas stove.

The students joined Mr. Miller and worked from 5 a.m. until midnight for three days to clean the filthy house. Furniture was provided. A registered nurse was sent out to talk to the older girls. The youngsters were bathed. Medical treatment was given. And after much pressure the farmer piped in cold water for bathing and gas for cooking —increasing the rent deduction from the meager paycheck.

Further pressure through church members on the farmer's wife over several months eventually produced a larger home for the family. And a Spanish minister began calling on the youngsters and soon they were attending church.

Special speakers brought in

The Scottsbluff-Gering Fellowship of Christian Athletes also has worked with children, as have other groups.

Three prisoners from Colorado have been flown in to speak to high-school groups on how to avoid a life of crime. Two nationally known speakers in the field also were brought in. Their talks were broadcast on the local radio station and picked up in schools throughout the area.

A community meeting was held by the advisory committee in the county jail. A display on drug abuse has been set up, and pamphlets distributed. A film on narcotics was purchased and has been shown across western Nebraska. "Shining Light" awards are given to those who contribute to delinquency prevention. Efforts continue to establish a big-brother and big-sister program for youngsters in need of a friend.

Efforts are being made to establish a halfway house for youngsters who cannot adjust to foster home living and cannot stay in their own homes.

Dependent and neglected youngsters are temporarily held in a shelter-care facility, rather than jail—the St. Christopher Child Care Center operated by the Order of Corpus Christi Carmelite Sisters. (Because of a shortage of funds and climbing costs, the center is reported to be in danger of closing.)

Jobs hunted down

The committee also tries to find jobs for youngsters. This is hampered by outdated child-labor laws designed to prevent exploitation of children and by the demise of the local Neighborhood Youth Corps unit.

Youngsters who are caught with alcohol in their possession are fined $100 and costs.

Other older youngsters may also be fined for certain offenses. All are permitted to work off the fines on community projects. Five youngsters are developing small islands in the river into recreation areas with the voluntary supervision of Earl Shultz, a local carpenter.

Other children make restitution for vandalism by working under adult supervision. One group of 7-, 8-, and 9-years-olds is cleaning up a construction company's yard. The youngsters had stolen radiators, spark plugs, and other parts to sell.

Since the only swimming pool is located in a middle-class neighborhood, city fathers have just agreed to build a second pool more accessible to the poor, says Mayor Thomas.

In the past, the police department has followed a policy of harassment of young people, the Mayor adds. But a bright young California officer with a degree in police science has just been hired as police chief. James A. Teal makes it clear that not only will he work with the juvenile advisory committee, but that he intends to give his men training and insight into better ways of handling youth.

Changes threaten leadership

Problems threaten to knock Scotts Bluff County from its status as a national leader in delinquency prevention. The county judge, Richard S. Wiles, has taken a state post in Lincoln.

The new judge, James L. Macken, who has been on the bench only a few days, admits that he is uncertain which direction he will go. Some fear he will be far more rigid and less imaginative than Judge Wiles, or fail to use the advisory committee properly. Yet Judge Macken says he "wants to learn," and is a "strong believer in probation."

Mr. Miller, probation officer, says he may quit, since his frequent requests for help have been turned down by the county board. Judge Macken replies that the decision on help for Mr. Miller is not final, but believes Mr. Miller is an outstanding juvenile officer and will urge him to stay.

Scotts Bluff County officials openly admit that many of their ideas are really not original. They give much credit to Boulder County, Colo., for pointing the way.

In recent years Boulder's juvenile court has gained national recognition for pioneering in the volunteer field and in opening Attention Homes for children in trouble — attention as opposed to detention.

Boulder court cooperates

Beyond this, Boulder has an outstanding year-round recreation program and a welfare department that not only is concerned about children in trouble — and doing something about them — but also is able to work in harmony with the juvenile court. (In Scottsbluff and in many other cities the court and welfare department are at odds.)

Boulder's widely copied volunteer program is an outgrowth of a project begun by a University of Colorado sociologist, Gordon H. Barker. In 1957 he began assigning university students to work in the reform school in Golden, Colo.

In 1961, Professor Barker and Boulder County Juvenile Court Judge Horace B. Holmes began using carefully selected students as volunteer probation officers, after learning of a Laurence, Kan., judge who used law students in this capacity.

(During this same period Judge Keith Leenhouts was also pioneering in the use of volunteers in court in Royal Oak, Mich.)

From time to time Boulder residents offered to help in the juvenile court. But it was a few days after the slaying of President Kennedy that Dr. Ivan H. Scheier, a psychologist specializing in testing, "numbed by the assassination" walked in, asking for something to do.

"I had read that Oswald [Lee Harvey Oswald, accused of assassinating the President] was in a juvenile court but that no one had any time to do anything for him," said Dr. Scheier.

Volunteer help welcomed

Judge Holmes and his wife, June, had known Dr. Scheier casually as a member of the same folk-dancing group. When Dr. Scheier volunteered, Judge Holmes knew how to use him. For he had long been concerned with the almost impossible job of helping children in trouble with the sketchy information provided by even the best probation officer.

Judge Holmes listed the questions he needed answered. Dr. Scheier used a short personality test to answer the questions. He now spends 20 to 30 hours a week without charge helping the court and supporting the volunteer movement.

Soon another psychologist volunteered to give children attitudinal tests.

Later, an optimetrist walked in and began to give free eye tests. He quickly found that roughly half of the children in court had eye trouble. Hearing tests were added. The third child tested had a severe hearing problem that neither he nor his parents were aware of.

Many children also are given reading and IQ tests, proctored by volunteer women.

When court officials became weary of dealing with dropouts, a volunteer tutoring program was launched. So far, 35 different jobs have been performed by volunteers.

College students continue to work as volunteer probation officers. Now adults from the community also serve in this capacity—giving youngsters far more attention than they might get from a professional.

Church program tried out

A church referral program was tried. It failed because ministers and other church people were too busy doing other things. Those ministers who did do a good job "were already involved" with children in trouble, adds Charles Cameron, chief juvenile officer.

In the past year youngsters caught shoplifting have been asked to provide a day's service for each dollar's worth of merchandise stolen. Children may work for the city, help in the halfway house for ex-alcoholics, or in the parks. So far no child in this program has repeated the offense. Work programs are being tried for other violations, but so far with less success.

A sociologist teaches a course in family living for older boys and girls who want to get married. Often these youngsters only want to escape from home.

A group of volunteers has planned "retreats" into the mountains for youngsters who have used drugs. Each group will have 15 boys and girls. Follow-up meetings are planned. This program has been put together by Mrs. Sharon Fenner, a probation officer.

While Boulder still has a cold, prisonlike jail for holding children for courts, it has three volunteer-supported Attention Homes for those either waiting placement in institutions or foster homes or for a crisis in their own homes to end.

Parsonage rented for $1 a year

These are older homes—the first was a Methodist parsonage rented for $1 a year —that blend into a neighborhood.

Young house parents are hired, often married college students, for $200 a month plus room and board. The program is built on trust of children in trouble.

During the school year they attend local public schools. They also are permitted to go to the store for a soft drink or personal need or a movie or some recreational activity without supervision.

A report published by the Office of Juvenile Delinquency and Youth Development, U.S. Department of Health, Education, and Welfare, points out that "behind the volunteer-powered Attention Homes and individual foster-homes programs in Boulder is a belief that much of juvenile 'acting out' behavior is, at least at first, a plea for help. . . ."

The report adds that "the problems of children brought before the court are the problems of the entire community and, sooner or later, must be solved by the community."

In the big, old red-brick Attention Home a few blocks from downtown Boulder I met Don, a 14-year-old who was quietly playing an Attention Home guitar in his room.

Don had been involved in a series of burglaries. His 18-year-old brother is already in the reformatory.

Don "hates" his stepmother, a woman who broke up his home by having an affair with his father several years ago. Now he refuses to live with her. Yet his own mother, who has been ill, cannot keep him.

Don likes living in the Attention Home, not only because of the house parents, but because his father, a middle-class businessman, was always too busy to take him to the places he now goes—horseback riding, rodeos, the YMCA, the swimming pool.

'Home life' described

Perhaps even better evidence of the value of the Attention Home came from Carlos, a 15-year-old who has been "running since I was 13."

Carlos' father is divorced from his mother. His stepfather, a man he liked, has passed on.

He shyly talks about how he and his sister dislike the men his mother brings home, and how he is disturbed because "some of them stay half the night with her."

Carlos first went to a boys ranch, but ran from there, too. He has been in several foster homes, but has run from all but the last one, which he had to leave when the husband and wife developed problems of their own.

One of Carlos's problems has been at school where Anglo children "make fun of you and make you feel left out." Carlos is Mexican American. He has not run from the Attention Home, although doors and windows are unlocked.

Several federal studies have been made. One shows that the Attention Homes save a minimum of 500 child-days in jail each year.

(Niagara County, N.Y., has also pioneered, with even greater success, the use of open group homes for holding children in trouble. The jail in Niagara Falls is used far less than that in Boulder.)

Public funds provided

Boulder County had a population of less than 75,000 in 1960. It has grown considerably since. Yet its welfare department boasts 60 foster homes, plus three group homes that can accommodate up to 14 children each. One group home has been going for 12 years, a second for 6 years, the third for 3 years. Thus, Boulder is years ahead of many small or medium-sized counties.

Those who run group homes are paid $227 per month per child plus complete medical care. Foster parents taking one or two children receive from $66 a month for infants to $115 for each teen-ager, with varying rates between, depending upon age. Youngsters in foster homes also are provided clothing and medical care.

As in many counties, however, they find it difficult to place teen-agers, especially those who have been to court.

Children with special needs are often sent to private institutions in Colorado and other states for help and care.

The Welfare Department also employs three full-time homemakers who deal with families in trouble—teaching mothers money management, how to feed their families nutritious meals, how to clean and care for the house and otherwise maintain their families. Group meetings also are being tried.

There are other programs that might well be adopted by welfare departments in other states.

In recent months the Boulder Welfare Department has been successfully using volunteers, says Lew Wallace, the department's Director of Public Welfare.

In fact, the use of volunteers is the Boulder story.

Information center opened

Dr. Scheier has opened a national information center in the basement of the courthouse. A federally financed study shows that volunteers — if properly used — do make an important impact on solving the problems of children in trouble.

From July 14 to 18 a national seminar on volunteerism will be held in Boulder. Other seminars have been held in the past, and the volunteer movement is rapidly spreading.

Not long ago a volunteer and information center was opened in downtown Boulder serving 35 community agencies. Both adults and young people are involved. They may play games with retarded or crippled children, teach art, music, drama. Some tutor. Others work with alcoholics, the elderly, and mental-health patients.

Men and boys serve as fix-it men — repairing buildings, radios, playground equipment, whatever needs to be done.

Other volunteers are being asked to provide transporation to the poor to the health center, welfare office, or wherever else they need to go.

Boulder County has a day nursery that cares for children from broken homes with working mothers, as well as others who require this kind of help.

While this kind of day care is still being talked about as new in many corners of the nation, it has been in operation since 1922 in Boulder. Mothers who can afford it pay a fee. But much of the cost is carried by the United Fund (the Red Feather drive) and by private donations. The program runs year round.

Boulder County has an outstanding recreational program. Not only are there two swimming pools, but the city has 8,000 acres of parkland, some of it in the mountains. More parkland is being added every year.

During the year 400 different recreational classes are offered, both in the parks and in the city schools, which remain open evenings. Both youngsters and adults can learn to draw, dance, bowl, play bridge, guitar and banjo, tennis, make pottery, play golf. The program also includes hiking, swimming, and a variety of other activities.

While small fees are charged, children on welfare have pass cards that are as "good as cash anywhere," says Paul Swoboda, superintendent of recreation.

Summer jobs provided

Each summer 100 boys, 14-16 years old, are hired to work four hours a day, five days a week, up in the mountain parks to construct trails, build foot bridges, and do other jobs.

Although pay is only 50 cents an hour, the youngsters get swimming passes, passes to the nine summer teen dances, and to other activities. Appreciation parties are held. The boys are also issued hard hats and tee-shirts.

In its fifth year, large numbers of youngsters, rich and poor, compete for the opportunity to take part.

Another group of youngsters — boys and girls 14-16—compete for volunteer jobs as water-safety aides. All must pass junior Red Cross life saving tests.

Still another group of 75 girls volunteer each summer as playground assistant leaders. These youngsters also are trained and after one year may qualify as playground leaders. The girls get the same pay—50 cents an hour—and benefits as the boys who work on the park trails.

Mr. Swoboda strongly opposes Little League and other sports because he "detests parents out there pushing their own kids." Only "one in five is qualified to coach anyway," he adds.

Thus a Young America program has been developed for youngsters in the 4th, 5th, and 6th grades. Experienced, paid coaches teach youngsters to play football, wrestling, gymnastics, track and field, and other sports. Every child—skilled or clumsy—plays half a game. Emphasis is on "fun, safety, basic knowledge of the sport, physical conditioning, and competition"—and in that order of importance.

$250,000 a year for recreation

Boulder, which has a population of between 50,000 and 60,000 (the 1960 census shows 37,718) spends $250,000 a year on recreation for children, adults, and senior citizens.

Boulder offers much, much more. One could devote a book to the things going on there.

Take Alex Warner, a youthful but retired English teacher from the University of Colorado. He is running year-around science classes for 15 to 20 "black, white, and brown" youngsters in a corner of an old Quonset hut used by an Office of Economic Opportunity community-action center.

Children bring in leaves, feathers, spiders, snakes, bones — anything that interests them. They go on field trips up the mountainsides. Mr. Warner encourages them to collect and work with "junk," styrofoam packing material, plastic or cardboard containers from the grocery store—whatever they find. A few days ago the telephone company gave him cable they no longer needed.

"We don't spend a cent on this project," he says. Nor is he paid for the many hours he devotes.

The material the youngsters bring in always leads to the excellent children's room at the large new library. Not only do children learn about natural science here, but they are "tricked into improving their reading," Mr. Warner laughs.

This is the kind of imaginative approach —like the efforts in Scotts Bluff and Boulder Counties, Hughson, Calif. (see June 2 article in this series), and the Michigan communities described in last Monday's article —that offers the most promise in dealing with children in trouble.

"Running since I was 13"

CHAPTER XV

You can help children in trouble

These articles has sought to alert citizens to the plight
of America's children in trouble. Neglect, brutality, and
ignorance too often push these youngsters into delinquency
This chapter lists more than 170 specific steps you can
take to end this appalling waste of young lives.

Tens OF THOUSANDS OF AMERICAN children need help. This series has sought to alert the nation to their plight. Many are locked in jails unfit for adults. Thousands more go on to reform schools and other institutions that hurt more than they help.

Large numbers — no one has counted — have parents who are alcoholics, are emotionally unstable, or otherwise incapacitated. Some youngsters have wealthy parents who are so busy being important they have little time for their offspring.

Millions of youngsters are growing up in filthy, destructive slums. Other children fall apart in inadequate schools or find their way into the prison system through the welfare department.

The causes, as we have shown, are manifold. But three conclusions have emerged from this study:

● The present system for helping children in trouble is failing.

● Millions of tax dollars are being squandered in the process.

● Children in trouble *can be helped* with concerned, compassionate citizen support.

This final article is devoted to what you —whoever you are— can do to end this national scandal.

Individual citizens

1. Provide a foster home for a child in trouble.

2. Offer your services to detention homes, courts, welfare shelters, child-caring institutions, prisons, jails—wherever children are being kept. But be willing to give your time regularly. Don't build a child up only to let him down. (Volunteer help is needed everywhere. Information on volunteerism is available through Dr. Ivan H. Scheier, Courthouse, Boulder, Colo.)

There are opportunities to help them

3. Take a child in trouble with you on your vacation.

4. Open your summer cottage to a probation officer, welfare worker, or others working with children when you are not using it.

5. Teach a child to play a musical instrument.

6. Teach a child an athletic skill.

7. Become a pen pal with a child in an institution.

8. "Sponsor" a homeless child locked up. Remember the youngster on holidays. Buy a little clothing when needed. Visit him, to assure him somebody cares.

9. Start discussion groups in your community on ways to help children.

10. Become a "listener." Children behind bars need someone who is trustworthy and neutral to sit and listen. This may lead to your helping the child when he is released.

11. Take a child or a group of boys or girls camping or on weekend nature hikes.

12. Hire a slum child to help you at home during summer vacation. (But do it in the spirit of teaching and helping, not of getting cheap labor.)

12. Teach girls how to knit or sew or cook in your home.

14. Help a boy build a boat.

15. Take children whose parents agree (and have no active religious affiliation) to church.

16. Offer to teach a girl on probation or in detention, grooming, make-up, hygiene, and other ways to be attractive.

17. Offer to mend clothing for small children held in detention or shelter care.

18. Read to children—either in your own home, in the detention home, or other facility.

19. Start a chorus or band in an institution or underprivileged neighborhood.

20. Conduct clothing drives for institutions that hold children.

21. Bake cakes, pies, cookies and other treats for children in trouble.

22. Take a boy fishing.

23. Teach a boy about motors, carpentry, aviation, painting — whatever hobby or skill you have.

24. Provide a welfare mother (who wants help) financial advice. Help her shop. Give her credit advice so she does not get taken by wheeling and dealing merchants.

25. Open a one-woman (or one-man) job service. Find jobs for children in trouble. Find young workers for those who need them.

26. Provide employment counseling: Teach children how and where to look for a job; how to fill out forms; how to dress, and other things a child needs to know. This may also involve helping a child discover his skills.

27. Tutor a child having trouble in school. For some, all you may need to do is listen to them read.

28. Become a teacher's aide in a school — taking attendance, grading tests, and doing other things that will permit the teacher to give more attention to a child.

29. Become a materials procurer: Call stores, industries, and others for good waste materials and equipment for arts and crafts projects, vocational training classes, and other projects.

30. Become a discussion leader. Invite groups of young people into your home—or meet with them elsewhere—to talk about things that concern them.

31. Collect books and magazines of interest to young people for use in institutions and distribution to families who have none.

32. Subscribe to a magazine or paper for a child who cannot afford it.

33. Become a court investigator. Judges need accurate data on children who have been found delinquent, but in too many courts there is no probation staff, or too small a probation staff to do the job. Volunteer to gather the information the judge needs.

34. Provide clerical help to courts, other agencies.

35. Become a juvenile court greeter. This is especially needed in larger cities where frightened parents and children may wait for hours in a crowded, impersonal, lobby. Answer questions, pass out court literature, even serve refreshments.

36. Provide a baby-sitting service for mothers who must go to court or other agencies dealing with one of her children. This can be done either in the courthouse or in your own home.

37. Provide transportation for mothers or children who require agency services.

38. Write (and encourage your friends to do the same) to governmental officials and demand changes wherever needed.

39. Become a community resources coordinator. Gather information on the various agencies and institutions in your area and either duplicate and distribute the information or accept telephone calls from parents or children in need of help.

40. Offer your services as a repairman. Fix toys and do other jobs for child-caring institutions.

41. Teachers, dentists, artists, musicians, architects, psychologists, psychiatrists, writers, and other trained professionals should volunteer to council, teach classes, tutor, and otherwise provide services for youngsters both in and out of institutions.

Parents

1. Give your children love—not just material things. No ingredient is more important than this, the experts agree.

2. Set a proper example. Children copy their parents. Youngsters are quick to see through adult sham and hyprocisy. They learn what is important and how to act by observing how you behave and act.

3. Teach your children to be obedient—but do it the right way. Hitting children is, according to some experts, a sign of parental inadequacy, even unbalance. Too often it only leads to trouble. Look for better methods of controlling children.

4. Care enough to establish some basic, clear-cut, reasonable rules. Be consistent in enforcing them. But don't make up so many rules that the child becomes either frustrated or immobilized.

5. Know your children. Listen to them. Respond appropriately. Keep communication lines open.

6. Recognize that children are not adults and cannot be expected to act grown up. Often they will do foolish things. Be patient, firm, understanding.

7. Find constructive ways to praise your child — but again be balanced. Nagging never helps, but unlimited praise loses meaning.

8. From the start make it clear to a child that you care enough about him to want to know where he is and what he is doing. Set regular times for meals and expect your child to come when called or, if he can tell time, be home at the appointed time. Understand that youngsters will test these and other rules, and that patient, calm insistence on their being followed at an early age will help prevent problems later.

9. Do not constantly entertain and fuss over your small child. Instead permit him to have quiet periods to draw, work with clay, leaf through his own books, make mud pies, and do other creative things.

10. Hold interesting discussions at mealtime, but do not fight, bicker, or thrash out family problems. One father suggested that each child give a brief report on something interesting while standing behind his chair after each meal—a tradition that produced a very skilled public speaker. Communicating with adults is a problem to be resolved for all young people.

11. Encourage a child to express himself in many ways— through music, art, discussion, reading, athletics. A child with many interests and opportunities to succeed has little time to get in trouble.

12. If a child steals, avoid preaching. Do not put on a hysterical show. Do not play detective. Simply state fact. Be calm and firm, explaining that the object does not belong to him and must be returned. Do not overpunish. Help the child understand that he is responsible for his actions. But avoid dire predictions or threats like "You'll end up in prison" or "you'll be the death of me."

13. Do not ask questions or put pressures on a child that will encourage him to lie. Avoid police-interrogation techniques. Listen to what the child is really saying when he lies, and try to find better methods of communicating. (Lying and other topics of interest are discussed in Dr. Haim G. Ginott's book, "Between Parent and Child," Avon Books, 959 8th Avenue, New York, N.Y. 10019, and in other books for parents.)

14. Use trips in the car, ball games, visits to a park, walks, shopping trips—every-day activities — to help a child understand and respect law and the rights of others:

Let small children help watch for stop signs or for stoplights to change from red to green, and explain how that keeps cars from getting tangled up at corners. Discuss —and obey—speed-limit signs and how laws help keep highways safe. As a child learns rules for a game, remind him that there are many rules of fair play all about us. Show your child how one cleans up after a picnic—even taking away debris left by others—because we respect the rights of the next people to use the spot. Shoplifting is a growing problem. Discuss how a storekeeper must charge for things he sells so that he will have a pay check like daddy's to buy things for his children.

15. Take an older child to the police station, a city council meeting, or to other governmental agencies and functions so the child begins to understand who makes rules and how they are enforced and changed.

16. Set aside times for vigorous family activities, as well as quiet periods for simplification of life (a walk in the park, for example), and provide children private opportunities to discuss problems.

17. Encourage children to bring other youngsters home with them — especially those with different cultural, religious, or ethnic backgrounds. Invite these children to dinner and take those with inadequate homes on family outings.

18. Notice and think about frequent examples of unnatural behavior that may indicate problems such as drug use. Be calm and steady, but take appropriate steps immediately to correct the problem. Your panic or otherwise inappropriate behavior may drive such a child into running away.

Police

1. Carefully test all officers on attitudes toward adolescents and minority groups. Screen out those with bad attitudes.

2. Give classes to all new officers in adolescent behavior. Require a high mark to pass.

3. Hold frequent in-service training sessions on teen-agers and how to deal with them for officers already on the force.

4. Return officers to neighborhood beats.

5. Increase police salaries so standards for policemen can be raised.

6. Sponsor Boys Clubs, Boy Scouts troops, and other similar groups.

7. Sponsor automobile clubs, drag races, and other auto-oriented activities.

8. Sponsor a Police Athletic League (PAL), a program run by volunteer officers and aimed at those young people on the edge of trouble.

9. Start a big-brother-in-blue-program. This would be related to the traditional Big Brother program, with individual officers taking a personal interest in boys who need adult guidance and friendship.

10. Sponsor summer camp programs, with policemen acting as counselors.

11. Start police clubs in local schools for youngsters interested in police work.

12. Start a youth patrol program, where older children interested in police work are trained by veteran officers to do specialized jobs. In some communities these groups have helped ease tensions and prevent violence. In other communities youngsters serve as information aides in neighborhoods. Still others do clerical work and other routine jobs.

13. Open neighborhood store-front offices for easy, nonthreatening, citizen access to police.

14. Hold regular discussion sessions where individual policemen either serve as leaders or become involved in give and take.

15. Sponsor drum and bugle corps, drill teams, and other similar groups.

16. Collect and distribute data on alternatives to jail or detention homes for children in trouble. Prepare a manual listing all community agencies and their services for children.

17. Urge local schools to adopt the University of Cincinnati school program to encourage understanding of law and law enforcement. (See Article 12 in this series.)

18. Take youngsters on patrol, as is done in St. Louis.

19. Have officers make regular visits to schools for assembly programs and to talk to individual classes.

20. Demonstrate police equipment and the positive side of the profession on elementary-school playgrounds. Give children a ride in police cars. Hold first-aid classes.

21. Assign officers to schools full-time to teach and counsel.

22. Give officers working in ethnic neighborhoods special courses to help them understand the group's culture, problems, needs. Require language training for those working among non-English-speaking groups.

23. Lock officers in jail or prison overnight, as a California chief does, and take steps to sensitize policemen.

24. Avoid bluster, unnecessary violence, cockiness, or displays of bravado. Follow the advice given in the King County, Wash., sheriff's department manual: "It is of the utmost importance that officer attitude, demeanor, and speech toward juveniles be civil and respectful, but at the same time firm."

Judges

1. Follow the Gault decision (affirming that children have the same legal rights as adults) where it applies—even if you disagree with it. Judicial scoff-laws are extremely poor examples. If you believe the Supreme Court is wrong, challenge it through lawful channels.

2. Attend the Juvenile Judges Institute at the University of Minnesota, or the one sponsored by the National Council of Juvenile Court Judges, held in Reno, Nev. (Enrollment is limited, so apply early.)

3. Form a statewide juvenile judges conference. Hold sessions that deal with more than social or court affairs. Bring in outside experts, including those from other professions and disciplines.

4. Read the book "Guides for Juvenile Court Judges," published by the National Council on Crime and Delinquency; the book "Gault: What Now for the Juvenile Court," published by the Institute of Continuing Legal Education, Ann Arbor, Mich.; and "Standards for Juvenile and Family Courts," published by the United States Department of Health, Education, and Welfare, Children's Bureau.

5. Require detention officials to provide a daily list of who is held, for what reason, and for how long. No child should be detained more than a few days in tight custody.

6. Walk through detention facilities regularly to make sure conditions are as they should be. Make surprise visits.

7. As judge, where possible and appropriate, provide the leadership needed to assure adequate staff, facilities, and placement alternatives.

8. Establish a juvenile court advisory council of citizens from all walks of life and backgrounds. From this council build volunteer programs, as discussed in Articles 13 and 14 of this series. No city is too large or too small for this.

9. Hire investigators or use qualified volunteers to help the court understand the problems and needs of each child who appears before you.

10. Provide for treatment of the child in his own home whenever possible. Find foster homes and local group homes as a second alternative. Except in extreme cases involving protection of society, have the courage to refuse to send a child to a reform school if you are certain that the institution damages children. Most do.

11. Do not *threaten* a child with probation, reform school, or other presumably beneficial treatment programs. Such threats undermine the programs. You wouldn't threaten a child who has reading problems with a reading clinic.

12. Do not give stern, wordy lectures to children in trouble. Most start out with an extremely low self-image and have been nagged with only negative results before they arrive in court. Most children say they are too scared or angry to listen anyway, so you are wasting your breath and impressing only yourself. Instead, discover the child's needs and find ways to meet these needs so that behavior and attitudes will be improved.

13. Recognize that, with few exceptions, parents and their problems result in problem children. Include parents in whatever treatment program is deemed necessary. Also realize that taking a child out of his own home may create additional problems, instead of solving the difficulty. Detention, foster homes, or institutionalization should be resorted to only if there is nothing at all to build on in the child's home.

Lawyers

1. Volunteer for service as counsel in the juvenile court.

2. Form groups like the Boston Lawyers' Committee (one of 25 branches of the Ford Foundation-funded Lawyers' Committee for Civil Rights Under Law and organized eight months ago to provide free legal aid to groups — rather than individuals — with urban or minority problems) to meet the problems of poverty and discrimination. Attack horrible juvenile institutions through law suits — class actions where possible — either to force changes or to have children removed because institutions are not providing services needed.

3. When authorized by a client, sue for civil damages when children are beaten or otherwise abused while in custody.

4. When authorized by a client, challenge holding of juveniles in jails. In at least one state such an action has been appealed successfully.

5. Give legal help to groups trying to establish nonprofit or tax-exempt status for child-caring facilities of agencies. Also help change ordinances and statutes to accomplish what is needed.

6. Be available for court appointment to represent children in divorce actions and custody disputes.

7. Be available to legal-aid groups to represent students without funds suspended or expelled from school.

Businessmen

1. Provide full-time and part-time jobs for young people in and out of school who need employment.

2. Provide counseling for youngsters still in school, especially those from poverty areas and boys without a father. Provide them with the adult attention and guidance needed to assure their confidence in the existing system.

3. Provide equipment, space, and skilled workers to train youngsters in work skills that are marketable.

4. Offer scrap materials and rejects to training schools, detention homes, and groups working with children. It is surprising what a creative person can do with what would otherwise be classified as waste. Wire, plastic, metal, wood, paper—all can be put to good use.

5. Sponsor a promising child from a poverty family who is in trouble or on the edge of trouble. Help him finish high school, trade school, junior college, or attend a university.

6. Open your parking lot after hours as a play area.

7. Use company vehicles during off hours to assist recreation departments, reform schools, and others working with children. One Scottsbluff, Neb., businessman made his light plane available for juvenile court business.

8. Donate used typewriters, outdated machinery, motors, and other equipment to agencies working with children.

9. Farm out piece work to groups working with children in trouble so that youngsters can earn money. (See Kalamazoo program discussed in Article 13.)

City officials

1. Examine priorities. Too often emphasis is on highways, parking lots, airports, and the like, while children—with no lobby—are shortchanged.

2. Enforce building codes—require slum landlords to upgrade rental property.

3. Tear down condemned buildings and wherever possible convert the land to tot lots and green spaces to make urban living more bearable.

4. Do not build high-rise housing projects—better known as "vertical slums." Public housing should be no more than two stories high, with adequate play space, parking, and access to laundry service, stores, and schools. No project should house more than a dozen families.

5. Build one swimming pool and adequate park space for at least every 10,000 or 15,000 residents. Locate pools in neighborhoods where poor families live—within easy walking distance. Provide bus service until additional pools can be built. Let children on welfare in free.

6. Provide year-round recreation programs for both children and families. Turn schools into community centers to be used evenings, weekends, and during vacation periods. (See Article 13 for Flint, Mich., model.)

7. Close off streets and make them into supervised play lots for a few hours each day when parks and vacant lots are not available. Mobile units filled with games, books, recreation equipment, and arts-and-crafts supplies should make daily rounds.

8. In winter in Northern cities block off streets for sledding; flood tennis courts for skating. Provide supervision and equipment for poor children.

9. Crowded cities with too few swimming pools should provide sprinkler systems that attach to fire hydrants on hot days.

10. Train and hire mature high-school students as playground-activities directors. The Boulder, Colo., program (see Article 14) is worth copying.

11. Light up play areas at night for basketball and other sports.

12. Hold year-round teen dances in school gyms, on tennis courts, or wherever appropriate.

13. Use volunteers or hire college students, even mature high-school students, as "pied pipers." Carrying a softball and bat, paper, crayons, paint and brushes, or a good supply of books, they can find groups of children wherever they congregate in a neighborhood and lead them into constructive activities. These roving recreational leaders can hold sidewalk art classes, encourage summer reading, tell stories, lead singing—get involved in regular camp activities on city streets.

14. Open volunteer - run day - care centers for working mothers, or to permit a mother with preschool children an hour or two of freedom each week.

15. Develop family day or overnight camps for the poor. While children are engaged in recreation, welfare mothers and others can spend part of their time learning skills, discussing nutrition, and other child needs and problems.

16. Provide group homes for children who cannot remain with their own parents.

17. Build attention homes and other alternatives to jails for holding children in trouble awaiting court hearings or placement in foster homes or institutions.

18. Start an employment program for all boys and girls 14 and over. Some could be used in parks, as in Boulder, Colo., and Salt Lake City. Referrals could come through the probation office, schools, or by children simply applying. Volunteers, a city agency, or private sponsoring group could help train youngsters, find existing job openings, and develop jobs that presently do not exist. Youngsters could work steadily for one firm or person or form a job pool on call.

19. Reevaluate realistically city or county job requirements in an effort to employ as many dropouts as possible. Such standards as high-school diplomas, age, height, temporary health problems, even physical defects need not be barriers for certain kinds of jobs.

20. Follow the lead of Junior Achievement programs and expand them to open store-front "factories" for young people to manufacture and sell items and provide services for a profit.

21. Run summer dramatic classes in slum neighborhoods.

22. Hold art fairs in conjunction with sidewalk or playground arts and crafts classes.

Legislators

1. Reduce the population in all correctional institutions to 150 or less.

2. Ban the use of physical punishment in institutions.

3. Ban the use of solitary confinement or group confinement and other inhuman treatment in institutions.

4. Require improved screening techniques for all employees in child-caring institutions.

5. Require frequent testing of employees —at least every six-months—to assure their fitness to continue in this difficult work.

6. Upgrade salaries, and provide a mandatory vacation every six months for those dealing with hostile or hyperactive children.

7. Provide trained investigators to make frequent surprise checks on all institutions and agencies dealing with children. These investigators should not answer to those who head the agencies they investigate.

8. Follow the California plan of paying state funds to communities that provide positive alternatives that keep children out of state institutions.

9. Use matching funds to subsidize local probation departments that add qualified workers.

10. Establish regional group homes throughout the state and in cities—at least one 10-bed home for boys for each 30,000 population group and one for girls for every 50,000 residents.

11. Open forest camps and other small, specialized institutions to reduce reform-school populations.

12. Provide scholarships for child-care workers who want to take appropriate courses.

13. Locate child-care institutions near universities whenever possible so they can make use of both student help and professional expertise.

14. Require all state mental hospitals taking children to have special, properly staffed, adequately equipped child-care units. Require a psychiatrist who specializes in children to examine all children before admission.

15. Adopt rigid new standards of admission for retarded children to all institutions and provide group homes and other specialized institutions for these youngsters.

16. Provide tax and other incentives for communities, groups, and individuals who wish to open institutions for children in trouble. Subsidize such institutions where possible—especially whose run by local governmental agencies.

17. Support and subsidize community recreation programs and green space.

18. Require all school districts to provide remedial reading programs at all school levels.

19. Raise the legal school dropout age to 18, at the same time financially encouraging creative programs for youngsters with school problems.

20. Grant extra funds to or otherwise support school districts that reduce their dropout rates.

21. Provide more vocational training programs for youngsters failing in regular academic programs.

22. Revise labor laws so that under certain circumstances boys 14, 15, and 16 can find work. Also provide an insurance program or other safeguards for the employer.

23. Make gathering of statistics on children in courts, on probation, in institutions, etc., mandatory.

24. Abolish jails as storage places for children. If use of jails for children cannot be abolished, limit the time a child can be held in jail to 24 hours. Limit time in detention prior to a court hearing to 10 days, and then only after a detention hearing with the youngster represented by a lawyer. Limit the time a child can be held in detention after a hearing to 14 days.

25. Provide state regional detention homes in rural areas.

26. Make it illegal to transfer a child from a reform school or other institution to prison or mental hospital without full legal safeguards.

27. Establish local or regional family service centers with all appropriate agencies—mental health, dental care, welfare, etc.—housed either under one roof or in one multibuilding complex.

28. Require that needed services be provided to every family where a child has been removed and placed in an institution so that the family will be prepared to better receive the child when he returns.

29. Require (and financially support) joint and seperate training sessions for police officers, judges, probation officers, institutional workers, and others working with children.

30. Change marriage laws, so that it requires at least as much thought to get married as to get a driver's license.

31. Change divorce laws, making an impartial investigation mandatory in all child-custody cases. Also require that a lawyer be hired to represent the children's interests in every divorce action.

The press

1. Avoid simplistic solutions and editorials that are based on personal opinion or prejudice rather than fact.

2. Inform the public about the kinds of children caught up in juvenile systems of justice. Too many are dependent or neglected.

3. Investigate all child-caring institutions in the community and the state. Expose the flaws and press editorially for change.

4. Educate the public on the need for alternatives to reform school.

5. Sit on and give your support to court advisory boards and other private and governmental institutions and agencies trying to solve the problems of children in trouble —as is being done in Davenport, Iowa, and Dallas.

6. Be concerned with what you advertise or promote. Consider the impact it will have on children. Broadcasters have a special responsibility since (a) disc jockeys and records are highly influential, and (b) television is often used as a baby-sitter, without parental screening of what is shown.

7. Judges who damage children through ignorance, stupidity, or malfeasance should be removed from office. Put pressure on the electing or appointing authority to bring this about.

⋆ ⋆ ⋆

These are only a few of the possibilities that should be considered. Many have been discussed earlier in this series.

The churches, for example, must find ways to reach young people who are "turned off" by church members' "worship," money, cars, houses, clothing, and status.

Many youngsters are convinced that divine service too often means public worship rather than daily service to mankind. Thus they see churches as rather hypocritical, middle-class social clubs rather than institutions able to deal with today's problems in a meaningful way.

Universities still are doing a poor job in the child and family field. All students—regardless of major—could be required to spend at least a semester working in this area, using whatever talents they have. This would not only meet many of the immediate needs, but produce the kind of leadership and understanding needed to resolve the nation's problems.

Sociology and other related subjects too often are presented in an extremely dull manner. Students become so bogged down in jargon that they miss the understanding they most need.

Education courses are often little better. Too many future teachers really learn nothing about helping children in trouble.

Nor is there much meaningful research in the field of human behavior and corrections.

In too many communities the YMCA has become a sort of country club for adolescents—financially excluding children who really need help. Boy Scouts and boys' clubs also too often fail to reach hard-core youngsters.

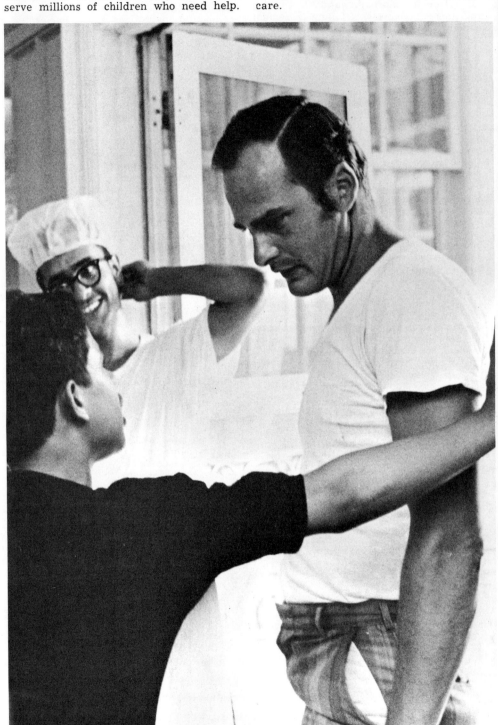

124

Experts agree that society's agencies and institutions must undergo critical self-examination to see how they can better serve millions of children who need help.

The problems of these children in trouble can be resolved. But not until the people of America understand them and begin to care.

Children in trouble _can_ be helped with concerned, compassionate citizen support

Photos by:

Gordon Converse * — pages 8, 32, 42, 54, 60, 116
Jim Hughes † — pages 28, 72, 100
Daniel Ilko — pages 108, 115
Howard James — page 1 opposite, pages 66, 102
John Littlewood † — pages 76, 82, 86, 124
Peter Main † — page 96
William Mares — pages 7, 15, 16, 20, 24, 36, 41, 50, 57, 68

* Chief photographer of The Christian Science Monitor
†Staff photographers of The Christian Science Monitor